Mindset matters.
*That is why Robert and Mickey's book is so eye opening and important for anyone who wants to take their performance to another level. Instead of treating mindset as a mystery, **The Power of Mindset Change** provides a way to map the three key levels of mindset and choose the focus that is most important for achieving your goals.*

– Internationally known speaker and *New York Times* Best
   Selling Author of *Life Force and Money: Master the Game*

*Mindset is a powerful concept that bridges the psychology of the individual and the collective. In **The Power of Mindset Change**, the concept is fleshed out with a comprehensive map of all the ways that one can drive excellence as an individual and as leader, and how Mindset connects and aligns these sources of success with goals and purpose. The book offers a powerful framework and practical tools to assess progress and provide coaching, and offers compelling examples from the lives of amazing people who have applied a conscious mindset practice in their careers.*

– CO-founder of *Siri*, developer in the area of humanistic AI and
   impact investor

*With **The Power of Mindset Change**, Robert and Mickey bring decades of research and experience to create a practical and insightful roadmap to improve personal performance. Most importantly, in this book they show how to measure and strengthen mindset in the areas that are most essential for achieving crucial goals.*

– Co-founder of the successful venture capital firm *Polaris Partners* and
   co-founder and vice chairman of the board of the *George Lucas
   Educational Foundation*

As an entrepreneur and CEO, I have used the MindsetMaps Inventory with my team and experienced the transformational power of understanding and adjusting mindsets. **The Power of Mindset Change** book is a unique and practical guide for those truly seeking to bring out the best in their teams and in each other.

Ludovic de Gromard

— Social entrepreneur, CEO and Co-Founder of *Chance*, digitally assisted career coaching services

Many authors promote the idea that "mindset matters" and most of us know from experience that they are right. But **The Power of Mindset Change** gives you in-depth insights into the 3 layers that actually foster your success, and an inventory to find out what you need to do to ramp up your own performance and joy. Robert and Mickey's model comes alive through the examples and stories they share. When you are ready to investigate yourself and learn to coach others through the process, this book can guide you to excel.

Shelle Rose Charvet

— Bestselling author of *Words That Change Minds* and international expert on the influence of language

The Power of Mindset Change

Why Mindset Matters Most.

By **Robert Dilts** and **Mickey Feher**

MindsetMaps International, Inc.
11 Saint George Rd
New York 11021.
USA

E-Mail:
Homepage:

I.S.B.N. 979-8-218186-64-7

TABLE OF CONTENTS

DEDICATION

To our children (Andrew, Julia, Abel and Simon)
who taught us so much about curiosity, mindset and fresh points of view.

To Robert's wife Deborah and Mickey's wife Bori,
who are relentless supporters and thought partners on our individual and
common journeys to illuminate our own mindset and help others to do the same.

To our community of MindsetMaps coaches and our clients
who have brought us many insights about the power of shifting mindsets
and the amazing results it can bring.

To Mickey's parents who after surviving the incredible cruelties of
Nazism prevailed under a Communist regime in Hungary and taught Mickey
to stick with passion and purpose no matter what happens around us.

To the power of mindset to create and support more hope,
empathy and meaning in healthy, happy and effective workplaces.

ACKNOWLEDGMENTS

We would like to acknowledge:

- Antonio Meza for designing the icons that make up the visual part of our MindsetMaps Inventory.

- Gerardo Gomez for the cover design and additional artwork.

- George Morvay and the team at Clay who created the first version of the web-based application.

- Simon Erdély and the team at Small Things whose technical competence has allowed us to take the online inventory to a next level.

- Our advisors Steve Arnold, Rob Feuer, Ludovic de Gromard, Tom Gruber and Robbie Steinhouse, whose invaluable support has helped us to continue to grow a successful international organization.

- Our partners and coach community who are working passionately to share the power of mindset change our world desperately needs.

- Our many inspiring role models who served as the foundation for the MindsetMaps Inventory. They are the giants upon whose shoulders we stand.

FOREWORD FOR MINDSETMAPS

Developing the *Success MindsetMap Inventory* (SMI) and the coaching process accompanying it has been a fascinating journey for both of us. Robert's odyssey began in the mid 1970s when he first met the founders of Neuro-Linguistic Programing (John Grinder and Richard Bandler) and understood the profound significance of mindset and mental programming on our lives. Since then, Robert has been studying the power of mindset to transform our lives, health, relationships, professional careers and collective potential. In 1999, Robert created the process of Success Factor Modeling with his late brother John to identify the "differences that make the difference" for highly successful individuals, teams and organizations. For many years, Robert did coaching, consulting and training for a wide variety of entrepreneurs and organizations (Apple Inc. was his first corporate client in 1980). These years of experience and research into what creates individual and collective excellence and success are a key part of development of the *Success MindsetMap Inventory* (SMI).

Our journey together began in 2013 in Budapest, when Mickey attended a program that Robert was giving on coaching and "The Hero's Journey." Mickey was a coachee for Robert during a demonstration of an alignment process focused on a set of distinctions that later became the foundations for what we call "Meta Mindset" in the Success MindsetMap. Mickey, who already had a successful coaching and training business in Central and Eastern Europe based in Hungary, experienced a significant breakthrough concerning his "big picture clarity" for the future and connected with an even larger vision and a sense of purpose. He realized he had a calling to take his work to a more global level and with a particular focus on being a bridge between cultures.

This breakthrough started an adventure in which our paths would continue to cross many times over the next decade in ways we could have never predicted. This journey included Mickey becoming an NLP Practitioner and getting his trainer certification at Robert's NLP University in Santa Cruz, California. Later, Mickey was the general manager of the International Association of Generative Change, founded by Robert and his colleague Dr. Stephen Gilligan. Since 2015, Mickey has been a member of the Dilts Strategy Group Success Factor Modeling[TM] Leadership Team. He has successfully taken his central European coaching and organizational development business to a global level and worked with many leadership teams of Fortune 500 hundred companies, training over 2,000 leaders and executives.

When Robert launched a major phase of the Success Factor Modeling™ (SFM™) initiative upon which this book is based, Mickey participated in a large modeling study of next-generation entrepreneurs, conducting in-depth interviews. During this period, in late 2014, the first seeds for the Success MindsetMap Inventory were planted. Mickey believed it was important to have a way to visualize the key qualities of a person's mindset. This idea intrigued us both, and we began to explore potential ways to do that. We initially envisioned a type of Internet game that would make a general categorization of the user's mindset, like the *Harry Potter Character Test* (https://www.idrlabs.com/harry-potter-character/test.php). This is from where the idea of using well-known entrepreneurs as iconic examples of specific mindset qualities originated.

As we developed the project further, we realized that there was potential for a very powerful tool, and the current version of the inventory began to take shape. Our interviews and studies of successful entrepreneurs and business leaders reached into the hundreds, and more and more key patterns began to emerge, especially in connection to building what is known as the Success Factor Modeling™ Circle of Success. This led us to make the distinction between Meta, Macro, and Micro Mindsets.

Our first version of what was to become the *Success MindsetMaps Inventory* (SMI) was a smartphone app. We enlisted Antonio Meza, who illustrated the three volumes of the *Success Factor Modeling* book series, to help us create the images and icons to be used for the map. We soon realized, however, that a phone app alone would be too limiting and tied to specific operating systems and switched to developing the web-based app that we use today. With the help of our developers at SmallThings, we set up a system that could be readily translated to other languages.

As we introduced the SMI to our clients and colleagues, it became evident that it was an extremely useful and powerful resource that provided a type of feedback and support that was unavailable in any other form. The ability to identify and shift patterns of mindset to reach desired outcomes provided key breakthroughs for our users that no other methodology could achieve. We originally intended the SMI to be like a mirror to users that would reflect key aspects of their mindset and offer them tips on how to enhance or improve areas of weakness. However, we began to realize that in the hands of trained coaches, the inventory could be a powerful

AI instrument of growth and transformation when linked to relevant professional development coaching tools and processes.

These realizations led to the creation of the twenty-page *Success MindsetMaps Premium Report,* which gives users and their coaches a detailed analysis of the different levels of the user's mindset and access to forty-nine unique online coaching tools designed to support the enhancement of specific qualities of Meta, Macro, or Micro Mindset. Our hands-on work with the SMI and Premium Report also provided the basis for the six-step *COACH+* process (described in chapter 10) for implementing the results of the SMI.

It is significant to note that the SMI and its related developments have all been generated as a result of practical application rather than theoretical speculation. The whole notion of a map of any kind is to provide the guidance needed to successfully navigate a particular territory. Thus, it has been important to us, at each step of the way, to make sure that everything we put in the MindsetMaps we apply to ourselves as well as to our clients. As we have built and grown MindsetMaps International, we have remained committed to practicing what we are preaching and "walking our talk."

In fact, it is this emphasis on practical applications that brought us to develop the twenty-eight-page *Success MindsetMaps Team Inventory Report* (summarized in chapter 12) and our forthcoming *Success MindsetMaps Conscious Leadership Inventory.* As we began to train MindsetMaps coaches and establish partners throughout the world, it also transpired that the SMI was not only valuable for entrepreneurs starting their own projects or ventures, but it was also a powerful resource for intrapreneurs working inside large organizations and business leaders of all types.

In the coming pages, you will learn more about all these developments. As you can see, our journey is well underway and is still in progress. We both consider the developments associated with the SMI to be part of a larger movement to bring greater awareness and transformation into the world of business. We hope you will find it as fascinating, exciting, and practically useful as we do and will consider joining us for more of this journey in the future.

Robert Dilts and Mickey Feher
Co-Founders, MindsetMaps International

AN INTRODUCTION TO MINDSET

Why do we say, "Mindset matters most"?

The power of mindset has been known for thousands of years. Great teachers, philosophers, and scientists alike agree that our mindset matters a lot. "Our life is the creation of our mind," said the Buddha, and "There is nothing either good or bad, but thinking makes it so," according to Shakespeare. "It's not what happens to you, but how you react to it that matters," said Epictetus famously.

Mindset seems to be at the epicenter of everything. It determines what we consider good or bad, whether we think a situation is unbearable or challenging, and how we respond to what's happening around us. But mindset is also a tricky phenomenon. It is often like being on autopilot, but without awareness of the program. An interesting example is a CEO client of Mickey's who likes to state that feedback is very important, yet, when it comes to critical moments, he absolutely shuts down and doesn't listen to anyone. However, when he feels business is going well, he asks for a lot of feedback, often from people with questionable expertise, and allows himself to be influenced. His goal is to scale his business, but his mindset seems to be a real obstacle with a constant change of direction. Another client, a senior leader, is looking for more satisfaction from her work. She has been with the same company for over a decade. Her mindset has created an impassable obstacle. She believes she can either choose to do the thing she loves and give up her financial security or do the work she hates and be secure. She says it feels like being on a leash and not being able to break free.

MINDSET IN SCIENCE

Though there seems to be a strong consensus about the significance of mindset, there are many questions about how to define it. According to Meier & Kropp, "A mindset is a mental attitude. It shapes our actions and our thoughts." According to Gollwitzer, it is "the sum total of the activated cognitive procedures." In this sense, mindset seems to refer to a set of beliefs or attitudes relative to some topic or object. This topic or object is often called the "attitude object." Most discussions about mindsets concern a specific attitude object (e.g., Dweck's growth mindset).

Researchers contend that mindset is a collection of beliefs, knowledge, attitudes, feelings, and emotions that one bears in one's mind regarding a certain issue at a certain time. This, in turn, shapes our thinking, feelings, and behavior. One example is when someone is in a good mood, they tend to be more altruistic than when they are in a negative or neutral mood. Another example is when someone believes that exam results are attributable to luck and not to intelligence or effort, they are inclined to study very little because they feel the results will not depend on the effort put in or the level of intelligence.

According to Festinger's cognitive dissonance theory, another strong characteristic of mindset is that humans don't like to maintain two attitudes and corresponding behaviors that contradict each other. When this is the case, people tend to change one of them, so the contradiction disappears. For example, if someone is a meat eater and thinks that eating meat causes cancer, they can either change their mindset to think that is not the case and hence keep on eating meat or move to a plant-based diet because they believe that meat-eating is indeed related to cancer.

The same applies to beliefs about climate change. If someone is a heavy environmental polluter, they are unlikely to believe in global warming and dangerous climate change. They will continue to not perceive their actions as a problem and believe that climate change is a hoax. If a person believes in climate change, they will change their habits and drive a smaller car or start using solar energy, etc.

Another interesting, related theory in social psychology is the notion of the "fundamental attribution error." This theory argues that the causes we attribute to our performance and behaviors, like internal vs. external, stable vs. unstable, controllable vs. uncontrollable, etc., greatly shape our performance and behaviors. For example, evidence shows that we tend to explain our failures (e.g., failing an exam) as a function of external causes (e.g., the exam was difficult) and our successes (e.g., performing well in an exam) as a function of internal causes (e.g., I performed well because I am intelligent).

MINDSET AS AN INNER ATTITUDE

Attitudes can be activated instantaneously but can be altered through cognitive processes. For example, when something is easy to understand and process, we like it. Conversely, new thoughts can trigger dislikes as people tend to strive for stability. Attitude also influences the way we store data. We tend to remember information about a subject that we appreciate more easily and in more detail than data about something we dislike.

Social psychologist Maio defines "... attitude as an overall evaluation of an object that is based on cognitive, affective, and behavioral information." The object of such evaluation can be material or immaterial. People build attitudes towards individuals as well as small, distinct groups (e.g., team members) or big, ambiguous groups (e.g., ethnic communities). Our attitude affects our perception of the evaluated object. Hence, we not only judge what is there but also change the information we gather and, in a loop, bias our evaluation of the object. For example, we often better remember people and information about objects and events that we like as opposed to people or objects we dislike or don't appreciate.

MINDSET AND PERFORMANCE

A tremendous amount of research links mindset and our inner attitude to performance. For example, attitude and creativity are strongly linked. Sternberg* describes "creativity as an attitude towards life" and lists various attitude-related methods to instill creative thinking. Kelley and Kelley* found that when people alter their attitude towards their creativity, e.g., they "improve their creative confidence" and make a conscious decision to be creative, they can improve their performance significantly and actually be more creative.

So, mindset can be viewed as a special kind of attitude. "A mindset is a mental attitude that determines how we interpret and respond to situations (Mehregany)."

We can also conclude that mindset influences the whole cognitive process, from perception to processing to storage and our affective state (French). It is, in fact, a cognitive orientation that determines how we handle a given task through a set of cognitive procedures (Achtziger & Gollwitzer).

As world-renowned Stanford University psychologist Carol Dweck maintains in her popular book, *Mindset: changing the way you think to fulfill your potential*, "a simple belief about yourself ... guides a large part of your life. ... Much of what may be preventing you from fulfilling your potential grows out of it."

MINDSET AND PERSONALITY

While there are some overlaps, mindset is distinct from personality. People with radically different personalities can take on the same mindset, while people with similar personality traits can adopt radically different mindsets.

How do we differentiate between personality and mindset?

According to the Encyclopedia Britannica, **personality** is defined as "a characteristic way of thinking, feeling, and behaving. Personality embraces moods, attitudes, and opinions and is most clearly expressed in interactions with other people. It includes behavioral characteristics, both inherent and acquired, that distinguish one person from another and that can be observed in people's relations to the environment and to the social group."

The word "personality" originates from the Latin word *persona*. "Persona" refers to a theatrical mask worn by performers to either project different roles or disguise their identities. Personality theories maintain that certain characteristic patterns of thoughts, feelings, and behaviors make a person unique. They believe that these unique characteristics remain consistent during our lifetime. Knowing these characteristics that define our unique individuality is helpful for self-awareness, which in turn helps us interact more effectively with others

However, when one studies the field of personality psychology, it quickly becomes clear that no definition of personality is universally agreed upon. There are several different schools of thought in and around psychology with their distinct definitions.

Humoral theories: some of the oldest known personality theories were described by the Greek philosopher Empedocles and physician Hippocrates. They maintained that humors were associated with variations in temperament like blood (sanguine), black bile (melancholic), yellow bile (choleric), and phlegm (phlegmatic). Such types of temperamental differences are typically present from birth, as even very young babies exhibit differences in terms of expressing emotions and whether they move a lot or are calmer and more motionless. These temperamental differences tend to be permanent and show up in later development stages as fundamental personality traits that do not change.

Psychoanalytic theories suggest that personality research should not only focus on studies of traits, attitudes, and motives but also on how personality develops over time. Freud and Jung maintained that personality characteristics are relatively stable over time and across situations and relate to certain motivations and traits. They also maintained that personality is affected by both biological and psychosocial forces that form our personality from early ages through social systems like family, school, and community.

Trait theories maintain that people differ from one another based on the strength and intensity of basic trait dimensions. Traits are people's characteristic patterns of thoughts, feelings, and behaviors, which are consistent and stable over time.

The best-known personality theory is the Five Factor Model (FFM), commonly referred to as the "Big Five" personality traits (McCrae & Costa) and recently popularized by Jordan Peterson. The big five are extraversion, agreeableness, conscientiousness, neuroticism (sometimes known by its polar opposite, emotional stability), and openness to experience (sometimes called intellect). Researchers have found that most people's big five scores remain relatively stable throughout their life. Other popular personality theories like MBTI, DISC, and PCM claim they can explain and predict a person's behavior in different contexts and they, and they also all claim that personality characteristics do not change significantly or at all over our life span.

As an experienced practitioner of personality theories, Mickey has often encountered interesting situations where two or more people had very similar personality structures in a team that he was working with, according to the personality assessment model he applied. Yet, those individuals behaved differently across several different contexts and circumstances. When studying these cases, he has concluded that these large differences ultimately relate to certain beliefs and other characteristics of mindset rather than to personality structures. Hence, mindset mapping combined with personality profiles can be a better predictor of decisions and actions than personality profiles alone.

MINDSETS CREATE FILTERS THAT ARE CONTEXT SPECIFIC

We know from neuroscience that mindsets "are lenses or frames of mind that orient individuals to particular sets of associations and expectations (Crum, Salovey, & Achor)." Mindsets help individuals make sense of complex information by offering them simple schematics about themselves and objects in their world.

One fundamental difference between personality and mindset is that mindset is domain and context-specific. We have different mindsets for different domains of our life and for different objectives. "Consistent with Dweck and Yeager's (2019) conceptualization of mindset, (test) results provide empirical support that mindsets are domain-specific and should be categorized at the characteristic adaptation level of personality." In short, mindsets may help or hinder us in achieving specific outcomes; therefore, our consciousness with respect to being in an appropriate mindset is crucial.

THE POWER AND CHANGEABILITY OF MINDSET

Mindsets can be life-changing. Another claim demonstrated by research is that mindsets help people organize their goals and have a strong effect on performance and higher goal achievement. "The way people organize their goals within the self-system, regulate their behavior and emotions in the pursuit of goals... is largely dependent on their mindsets, with a more growth mindset typically predicting higher goal achievement (Dweck and Leggett, Dupeyrat and Mariné)."

In her pioneering work, Caroll Dweck has shown how a fundamental belief related to talent can influence our whole life stance and whether we reach our full potential. She has identified the existence of a growth mindset and a fixed mindset. People with a growth mindset appreciate challenges and feedback and view this as an opportunity to learn. People with a fixed mindset see talent as something you either have or do not and therefore dislike new challenges and receiving developmental feedback.

In summary, mindsets:

- function as internal filters and influence perception, processing, and storing information in our memory
- are related to cognitive and emotional processes
- can operate as a blind spot and cause distortion if not correctly identified
- can be altered in response to certain situations and in relation to goals
- are strongly connected to our belief system, and we "hold" these in the form of a story in our minds.

Success MindsetMaps are a product of the process of SFM™. This unique research process was originally developed by Robert and John Dilts as a method of identifying and transferring the critical success factors necessary to promote the growth and impact of individuals, teams, and organizations, and to help them be optimally prepared to create, recognize, and take advantage of opportunities when they arise. By examining successful businesses, projects, and initiatives and observing the behavior of high-performing individuals and teams, SFM™ helps people and organizations quantify the key factors that create success and identify the trends necessary to extend that legacy into the future.

Success Factor Modeling™ is founded upon a set of principles and distinctions that are uniquely suited for analyzing and identifying crucial patterns of *business practices* and *behavioral skills* used by successful individuals, teams, and companies. The SFM™ process is applied to identify the critical success factors employed by successful entrepreneurs, teams, and business leaders and then to define specific models, tools, and skills that can be used by others to greatly increase their chances of producing impact and achieving success.

SFM™ involves observing and mapping the crucial mental and behavioral patterns that underpin exceptional performance. The goal of Success Factor Modeling is to identify the essential elements of thought and action required by an individual or group to produce a particular desired state or outcome, i.e., discover *"the difference that makes a difference."* It is the process of taking a complex performance or interaction and breaking it into small enough chunks that it can be recapitulated in some way. Success Factor Modeling then seeks to identify the *"pattern that connects"* those significant differences. The purpose of this process is to create a pragmatic map or "model" of some pattern of behavior that can be used to reproduce a similar degree of that performance by anyone who is motivated to do so. Thus, it involves benchmarking behaviors and ideas, as well as business practices and goals.

Success Factor Modeling can be likened to identifying the particular key needed to unlock the door to success for various life situations. Life circumstances present us with doorways leading to different areas of success. The locks on these doorways are the critical issues and contextual constraints we must address to reach our goal in those particular circumstances. The "key" to a particular "lock" is the appropriate combination of behaviors and the corresponding mindset required to effectively address the issues and constraints presented by a certain context.

A key that successfully unlocks one door will not necessarily unlock another. Thus, to address changing contexts, an effective model would include not only a description of the key but also one of the lock that the key fits.

An effective model provides a description of the lock (strategic goals and challenges) and the key which opens it (mindset and actions).

Thus, the objective of the Success Factor Modeling™ process is to make an *instrumental map* supported by a variety of exercises, formats, and tools that allows people to apply the factors that have been modeled to reach key outcomes within their chosen context. To accomplish this, SFM applies the following basic template:

PRODUCES

CREATES

The basic Success Factor Modeling template

Our *mindset*, which is made up of our inner state, attitude, and thinking processes, produces outer behavioral *actions*. Our mindset determines what we do and the type of actions we take in a particular situation. These actions, in turn, create *outcomes* in the external world around us. Achieving desired outcomes in our environment thus requires the proper mindset to produce the necessary and appropriate actions.

Thus, desired outcomes are the "locks" an individual is seeking to successfully open. An individual's mindset and actions form the "key" that will open a particular lock. The goal of Success Factor Modeling is to find the proper "keys" which open the "locks" necessary to reach our desired outcomes.

Success Factor Modeling maps the "differences that make the difference" in producing an effective performance.

THE SFM CIRCLE OF SUCCESS™

For several decades, Success Factor Modeling methodology has been applied to study hundreds of successful entrepreneurs and business. These studies have led to the formulation of the *SFM Circle of Success™*. Through these studies and interviews, we have discovered that the founders of successful companies divide their focus of attention evenly between five fundamental perspectives: 1) themselves and their passion for what they are doing, 2) their vision for their customers and their products and/ or services, 3) their investors and stakeholders, 4) their strategic partners and alliances, and 5) their team members or employees.

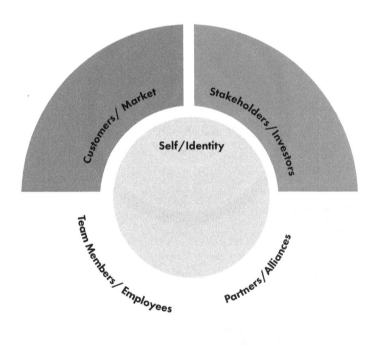

The basic elements of the SFM Circle of Success™

To survive and flourish in their projects and ventures, effective entrepreneurs and business leaders need more than a good product or service that is attractive to potential customers. They must also be sufficiently supported by team members, investors, alliances, and strategic relationships. As one successful entrepreneur put it, "You have to work with everybody, every day, your employees, your investors, your customers, and your partners, to bring your vision together."

We have found that effective entrepreneurs build and apply their Circle of Success to achieve five core **outcomes**: 1) personal satisfaction, 2) meaningful contribution, 3) innovation and resilience, 4) scalable growth, and 5) financial robustness.

These outcomes are achieved by combinations of *actions* related to the various parts of the Circle of Success.

- Attaining **personal satisfaction** comes from (a) *connecting to purpose and motivation*.

- The outcome of **meaningful contribution** is primarily achieved through the actions of (b) *developing a product or service* that benefits customers and (c) *creating alignment* among team members to support that development.

- Achieving **innovation and resilience** is fundamentally a consequence of the actions of (d) *increasing the competency* of one's team members and (e) *enriching and leveraging resources* through partnerships and alliances.

- The outcome of **scalable growth** is predominantly achieved through the actions of (f) *building win-win relationships* with partners and allies and (g) *expanding the business and creating value* for stakeholders and investors.

- **Financial robustness** is largely the result of the actions of (h) *raising investment and acquiring essential resources* from stakeholders and investors and (i) *generating interest and revenue* from customers.

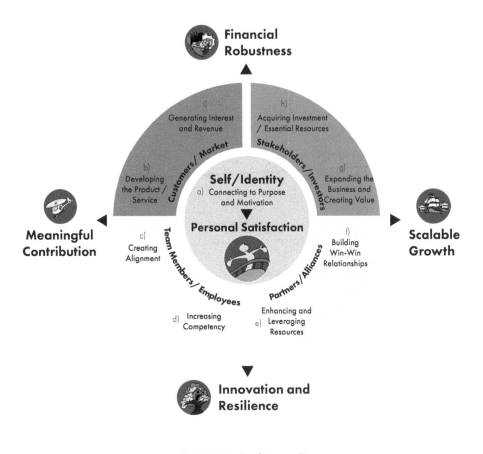

The SFM Circle of Success™

THE SUCCESS MINDSETMAP™

A major mission of Success Factor Modeling is to help entrepreneurs and conscious leaders of all kinds build an effective Circle of Success. As part of this mission, the authors, with the support of SFM illustrator Antonio Meza, have developed what we call the *Success MindsetMap™*.

To create the map, we have applied the principles of Success Factor Modeling to analyze well-known entrepreneurs like Elon Musk of *Tesla* and *SpaceX*, Steve Jobs of *Apple Inc.*, Richard Branson of the *Virgin Group*, Jeff Bezos of *Amazon.com*, Howard Schultz of *Starbucks*, Muhammed Yunus of *Grameen Bank*, Anita Roddick of *The Body Shop*, and many others. We have established several specific patterns of mindset that are shared by the most successful entrepreneurs and business leaders.

As defined in the previous chapter, our Success MindsetMap™ identifies three main areas of a successful mindset:

1. **Meta Mindset** – big-picture clarity.
2. **Macro Mindset** – habits of success.
3. **Micro Mindset** – ongoing priorities.

Meta Mindset is about our fundamental attitude toward our work, our world, and our place in that world. Meta Mindset relates to success factors at the levels of *purpose* and *identity*. Our Meta Mindset is essentially made up of our sense of passion, vision, mission, ambition, and role. These provide the *big picture clarity* concerning our project or venture.

Macro Mindset relates to the mental disciplines and practices required to bring focus to our venture's big picture and begin to put it into action. These practices and disciplines involve success factors at the level of *capabilities* like managing our energy and focus, seeking honest and frequent feedback, scanning for opportunities, dealing effectively with risks and adversity, and recharging and balancing ourselves. In this sense, our Macro Mindset defines our *habits of success*.

Micro Mindset produces and guides the specific actions necessary to build a sustainable venture. Micro Mindset focuses on success factors at the level of *behaviors*. It determines our *ongoing priorities* like clarifying purpose and motivation, developing our product or service, generating interest and revenue, growing and aligning an effective team, acquiring necessary resources, expanding our business, creating value for stakeholders, and building win-win partnerships that enrich and leverage available resources.

These three areas of mindset may be integrated together to make what we call the "Success MindsetMap™." The fundamental notion of the *Success MindsetMap™* is that particular aspects of mindset are more necessary to achieve the various core outcomes defined by the Circle of Success than others. Securing financial robustness, for instance, would require a different combination of Meta, Macro, and Micro Mindset attributes than would be necessary for, say, increasing innovation and resilience. Thus, like a literal map, the Success MindsetMap™ shows which course to take if you want or need to move your project or venture in a certain direction.

Meta Goals

A Meta Goal is a current focus of a project or venture. There are many important goals that people are probably working on, but the meta goal is the most vital one for the ongoing context.

The Meta Goal or current focus will relate to one of the five core outcomes associated with building a Circle of Success:

Increasing personal satisfaction. To symbolize this goal, we have chosen a person standing with arms outstretched on the bow of a ship like the famous scene from the movie *Titanic*. It represents a sense of joy, excitement, and pleasure in one's ongoing actions and activities. A person or team will choose this goal if things are going fairly well in their project or venture, but they want to be more enthusiastic and excited about what they are doing.

Making a genuine and meaningful contribution. We have selected a rescue helicopter to represent this goal as it symbolizes a clear focus on serving others. A person or team will choose this goal if it is important for their project or venture to clarify and/or enhance the benefit they are bringing to or creating for their customers and community.

Achieving greater innovation and resilience. We have chosen a tree house like that of the Swiss Family Robinson to represent this goal as it symbolizes ingenuity and the ability to adapt creatively to new and challenging situations. A person or team will choose this goal if they need to increase their capabilities or creativity to get through a crisis, deal with a big change, or stay competitive.

Establishing financial robustness/profitability. We have selected a treasure chest to represent this goal as it symbolizes a robust financial state. A person or team will choose this goal if it is essential for their project or venture to achieve profitability or financial stability.

Building a scalable business. We have chosen a fleet or armada to represent this goal as it symbolizes an expanding group of units operating together and sharing a common origin, purpose, and mode of coordination. A person or team will choose this goal if it is important for their project or venture to expand and grow.

Building the Map

In summary, Success MindsetMaps™ specify which elements of the three areas of mindset, Meta, Macro, and Micro, are most important and relevant for achieving the various core outcomes defined by the Circle of Success. Depending on your *Meta Goal* or *current focus* for your venture, that outcome could be enhancing personal satisfaction, making a meaningful contribution, securing financial robustness, increasing innovation and resilience, or achieving scalable growth. The Success MindsetMap™ helps you identify your particular aptitudes and tendencies and to know which ones you need to prioritize and strengthen to take your project or venture to the next level.

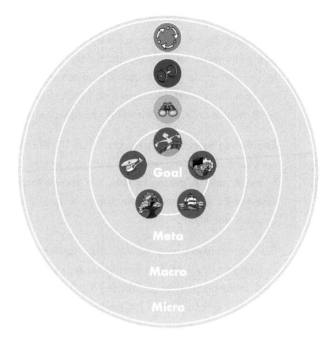

The Success MindsetMap identifies the key areas of Meta, Macro and Micro
Mindset needed to achieve a particular goal

In the coming chapters, we will go into more depth about each of these mindset
areas, illustrating them with case examples and showing how they can be applied
to building a robust and sustainable Circle of Success.

META MINDSET
– BIG PICTURE
CLARITY

Meta Mindset relates to success factors at the levels of *purpose* and *identity* and is about your fundamental attitude toward your work, the world, and your place in that world. To help clarify and enrich each element of Meta Mindset, we have selected quotes from well-known entrepreneurs who typify the various aspects of Meta Mindset and provide a type of iconic reference point.

Starting or building a project or venture is very much like the journeys taken by the early explorers. They needed a certain mindset and set of tools to arrive at their desired destinations. We have also chosen to use several legendary explorers, navigators, and leaders, like Ulysses, Ernest Shackleton, Christopher Columbus, Sir Francis Drake, Admiral Horatio Nelson, and Noah, to symbolize key aspects of the Meta Mindset of successful entrepreneurs and business leaders.

The Meta Mindset of successful entrepreneurs and leaders is made up of the following six elements:

1. PASSIONATE:
Know what you really love to do
(know what you are passionate about).

Passion is an intense desire or enthusiasm for something. It is a relentless inner drive to find what you care deeply about and for which you have talent and pursue it with all your heart. Our symbol for passion is the *spark* that ignites the fire of your enthusiasm, determination, and energy for making a difference.

You need passion and energy to create a truly successful business.

There is no greater thing you can do with your life and your work than follow your passions in a way that serves the world and you.

— Richard Branson – The Virgin Group

We have chosen entrepreneur Richard Branson as the role model for passion in business. Acknowledged as a passionate and inspiring leader, Branson is best known as the founder of the Virgin Group, which comprises more than 400 companies. On starting his businesses, Branson claimed, "My interest in life comes from setting myself huge, apparently unachievable challenges and trying to rise above them ... from the perspective of wanting to live life to the full, I felt that I had to attempt it."

We have selected the famous mythical traveler Ulysses as our other role model for passion. In the works of Homer, Dante, and Tennyson, Ulysses is depicted as a passionate voyager who "lusts for adventure." In the *Odyssey*, Homer's Ulysses fervently states, *"The journey is the thing."* Claiming that, "Each man delights in the work that suits him best," Ulysses declares: *"Let me not then die ingloriously and without a struggle, but let me first do some great thing that shall be told among men hereafter."*

According to Tennyson's Ulysses, "I cannot rest from travel: I will drink Life to the lees [the sediment at the bottom of the bottle]; all times I have enjoy'd greatly, have suffer'd greatly, both with those that loved me, and alone."
He claims that he is driven by the desire "to strive, to seek, to find, and not to yield."

— Ulysses

To explore this aspect of your Meta Mindset, reflect upon how clearly you can answer the following questions:

- *What do you really love to do?*
- *What are you excited about?*
- *What is interesting and compelling for you?*
- *What brings you a deep sense of enthusiasm and energy?*

2. VISIONARY, 2/1:

Know what you want to help create in the longer-term future (are clear about your destination and your longer-term vision).

Vision can best be defined as "a mental image of what the future will or could be like." The creative vision of successful entrepreneurs is about this ability to imagine and focus on longer-term possibilities that improve our lives in some way. It involves the ability to see beyond the confines of the "here and now" and imagine future scenarios. It also involves the capacity to set and stay focused on longer-term goals, adopting long-term plans and a holistic view. Our symbol for this type of vision is a *map* that shows the destination you are attempting to reach.

We are stubborn on vision. We are flexible on details... Amazon.com strives to be the e-commerce destination where consumers can find and discover anything they want to buy online.

— Jeff Bezos – Amazon.com

Jeff Bezos, founder of the Internet e-commerce giant Amazon, is our role model for vision. Bezos claims he left his "well-paying job" at a New York City hedge fund when he "learned about the rapid growth in Internet use" in the United States. He saw this as a major opportunity for people to have easier access to products, initially books, and pay less because they did not have to pay taxes on online purchases. He launched Amazon.com in 1994 after driving cross-country from New York to Seattle, writing up the Amazon business plan on the way. Like other budding entrepreneurs, he initially launched his vision from his garage. By 2014, Amazon had become the world's largest online retailer.

I made a vow to myself that someday, I would go to the region of ice and snow and go on and on till I came to one of the poles of the Earth, the end of the axis upon which this great round ball turns.

— Ernest Shackleton

Sir Ernest Henry Shackleton was a polar explorer who led three British expeditions to the Antarctic. As a result of his relentless pursuit of his vision, Shackleton was the first person to see and travel on the South Polar Plateau. Shackleton's self-sacrificing leadership and determination to reach his destination against all odds made him one of the principal figures of the period known as the Heroic Age of Antarctic Exploration.

To explore this aspect of your Meta Mindset, reflect upon how clearly you can answer the following questions:

- *What do you want to create in the world through you that is beyond you?*
- *What new possibilities do you want to see in the world?*
- *What is the world to which you want to belong?*

3. VISIONARY, 2/2:

Are clear about your direction, regardless of whether you know the ultimate destination.

Vision is about looking into the future to see what you want to create in the world through your venture. When you look far away, however, you cannot always see the result so clearly. Sometimes, an entrepreneur has a direction in mind but *not a* specific end goal or destination. Entrepreneurs like Jeff Bezos were very clear on their destination. Others like Anita Roddick knew their direction but not the ultimate destination.

We have chosen a *compass* to represent this type of vision in which you know which direction you want to go but not necessarily where you will end up.

You can create an honorable livelihood, where you take your skills and use them, and you earn a living from it; it gives you a sense of freedom and allows you to balance your life the way you want.

Crazy people see and feel things that others don't. But you have to believe that everything is possible. If you believe it, those around you will believe it too.

— Anita Roddick – The Body Shop

Anita Roddick was a British businesswoman, human rights activist, and environmental campaigner, best known as the founder of *The Body Shop*, a cosmetics company producing and retailing natural beauty products that shaped ethical consumerism. The company was one of the first to prohibit the use of ingredients tested on animals and one of the first to promote fair trade with third-world countries.

Roddick, however, initially just wanted to create a livelihood for herself and her daughter. She also believed that the world needed to "Go Green," as she put it. Based on her early travels around the world, she kept asking herself, "Why waste a container when you can refill it?" "What if you could build a venture that is based on a green philosophy and fair trade?" Roddick claimed she had no clue how she built a corporation that "is a multi-local business with over 2,045 stores serving over seventy-seven million customers in fifty-one different markets in twenty-five different languages and across twelve time zones." She clearly had the "compass" but not the map with the exact destination.

I am not solicitous to examine particularly everything here, which indeed could not be done in fifty years because my desire is to make all possible discoveries.

— Christopher Columbus

Christopher Columbus is the iconic example of a traveler who was clear about his direction but had no real idea of exactly where it would lead him and his crew. Convinced that the Earth was spherical and that he could reach the East Indies by sailing west for long enough, Columbus used a compass to stick to his magnetic westward course for weeks at a time. By doing so, he ended up discovering a whole new world unknown to Europeans of the time and launched the beginning of the European exploration and colonization of the American continents.

To explore this aspect of your Meta Mindset, reflect upon how clearly you can answer the following questions:

- *What do you want to see better or different in the world?*
- *What do you want to see more and less of in the future?*

4. PURPOSEFUL:

Know your purpose; know what you stand for and why you are doing what you are doing; are clear about your mission; the unique contribution you want to make through your venture.

The mission of an individual or organization is about their contribution to manifesting a particular vision. The word comes from the Latin *missio*, which means "the act of sending." In fact, mission is defined in the dictionary as "an important assignment carried out for political, religious, or commercial purposes." Mission relates to the unique gift and contribution that you bring to the table as you set out on your journey to realizing your vision. Similarly, an organization's mission will be with respect to the larger system of its customers and their needs.

We have selected a *barrel* as the symbol for purpose and *mission* as *it represents the cargo you are bringing to others to make a positive difference* in their lives.

Making money is a happiness.
And that's a great incentive.
Making other people happy is a super-happiness.

— Muhammed Yunus – Grameen Bank

Muhammed Yunus is a powerful role model for a sense of purpose and mission. He is the founder of Grameen Bank, which pioneered the concept of microcredit for supporting entrepreneurs in developing countries (see *SFM Vol. I, pp. 66-67*). Yunus' vision emerged when he discovered that very small loans could make a huge difference for people who had scarce economic resources. In his native country of Bangladesh, for instance, Yanus observed that village women who made bamboo furniture struggled to keep their small businesses going and were often taken advantage of when they tried to borrow money. Traditional banks did not want to make loans to poor people due to what they perceived as the high risk of default. Yunus, however, was convinced that, given a chance, the women would be more than willing to repay the money and a reasonable amount of interest. Yunus lent $27 of his own money to forty-two women in the village and made a small but significant profit on every loan. This validated his vision and reinforced his belief that microcredit was a viable business model that could positively transform the lives of people living in poverty.

On 1 October 1983, Yunus launched a full-fledged bank for poor Bangladeshis named Grameen Bank ("Village Bank"). By July 2007, Grameen had issued $6.38 billion to 7.4 million borrowers. In 2006, Yunnus and Grameen Bank received the Nobel Peace Prize for these efforts, the success of which has inspired similar programs throughout the world.

A great flood is coming. The waters of the heavens will meet the waters of earth. We build a vessel to survive the storm. We build an Ark.

— Noah

Noah is the Biblical character who built a gigantic vessel (an Ark) to save the animal species of the Earth (gathering them two-by-two) from being wiped out because of a vast flood. Clearly, Noah represents a traveler with no particular direction or destination but rather has a strong mission and purpose, the preservation of terrestrial life on Earth. As a role model, Noah diligently accepted his calling to serve something bigger than himself and never wavered from it.

To explore this aspect of your Meta Mindset, reflect upon how clearly you can answer the following questions:

- *What is your service to the bigger system and vision?*
- *What is your unique contribution to making the vision happen?*
- *What are the special gifts, resources, capabilities, and actions that you bring to the larger system to help reach the vision?*

5. AMBITIOUS:

Are clear about your ambition; what you want to become and achieve in the next two to five years.

Ambition is the result of your desire and determination to achieve success and recognition for yourself. Ambition is defined as "a strong desire to do or to achieve something, typically requiring determination and hard work" that brings you personal benefit. Your ambitions in the form of dreams and aspirations for your life arise from a healthy ego and come from your drive for growth and mastery. Ambitions arise from your personal dreams, desires, drives, and needs. In addition to making a reasonable or good living from your endeavors, for example, you may have a desire for growth, a drive for achievement, or a need for recognition and approval.

We have chosen a *timer* as the symbol of ambition for two reasons. *First, it represents a type of "race against time," an attempt to achieve something within a defined period. Second, it indicates the notion that, as Steve Jobs pointed out, our "time is limited," and it is important to stay focused on your goals and aspirations.*

We're here to put a dent in the universe. Otherwise, why else even be here? Our goal is to make the best devices in the world, not to be the biggest. Your time is limited, so don't waste it living someone else's life.

— Steve Jobs – Apple Inc.

In many ways, Steve Jobs is the epitome of entrepreneurial ambition (see *SFM Vol. I*, pp 252-280). Jobs founded Apple Computer with Steve Wozniak in a garage in Silicon Valley in the San Francisco Bay Area, California, in 1976, at the age of 21. When the company went public in 1980, it generated more capital than any stock market launch since the Ford Motor Company in 1956 and created 300 new millionaires overnight. By the time of Jobs' death in October 2011, Apple had become the largest technology firm in the world, with revenue for the year of $127.8 billion in sales. In March 2012, its stock market value reached $500 billion. In January of 2022 Apple became the first company ever to reach a $3 trillion market valuation.

Disturb us, Lord, when we are too pleased with ourselves when our dreams have come true, because we dreamed too little when we arrived safely. Because we sailed too close to the shore.

Disturb us, Lord, to dare more boldly, to venture on wilder seas where storms will show Your mastery; where losing sight of land, we shall find the stars.

– Sir Francis Drake

Sir Francis Drake is a vivid role model for a bold and ambitious adventurer. An English sea captain, privateer, navigator, and politician of the Elizabethan era, Drake carried out the second circumnavigation of the world in a single expedition from 1577 to 1580. His incursion into the Pacific also initiated an era of privateering and piracy against the Spanish on the western coast of the Americas. He was second-in-command of the English fleet that defeated the Spanish Armada in 1588. The most renowned British seaman of his time, Drake was awarded a knighthood in 1581 by Elizabeth I.

To explore this aspect of your Meta Mindset, reflect upon how clearly you can answer the following questions:

- *What type of life do you want to create for yourself?*
- *What do you want to accomplish? What type of status and performance do you want to achieve with respect to yourself and others?*
- *What would you like to be recognized and/or remembered for? What would you like to add to your resume or biography?*

6. ACCOUNTABLE:

Are clear about your role; the position you have with respect to others in your market/environment.

Role is defined as "the function assumed or part played by a person in a particular situation." Thus, roles are related to both "function," which is based upon competency, and "the part played," which is determined by position or status. So, on the one hand, a role reflects personal skills, abilities, and effort. It is related to what a person does or is expected to do. In fact, people are most successful in roles that are "compatible with their personal characteristics and skills." On the other hand, role reflects "status," i.e., who a person is in relation to others. In other words, role is an intersection of both the position a person occupies with respect to others and the expected capabilities and behaviors attached to that position.

We have selected a *flag* as the symbol for role as flags themselves are most often used as potent symbols representing role, status, or identification with a particular function or identity.

Starbucks has a role and a meaningful relationship with people that is not only about the coffee.

—Howard Schultz – Starbucks

Starbucks has become ubiquitous around the world as a brand that represents a particular role known as "coffeehouse culture." Dating back to the 14th century, coffeehouses in Western Europe and the Eastern Mediterranean were traditionally social hubs and artistic and intellectual centers. Howard Schultz had a vision to bring the role and tradition of the Italian coffeehouse to the United States, making it "a place for conversation and a sense of community; a third place between work and home." Embracing this role, Schultz set out to make Starbucks a different kind of company. One that not only celebrated coffee and rich tradition but that also brought a feeling of connection. Today, Starbucks is considered the main representative of "second wave coffee" and operates 23,768 locations worldwide in more than seventy different countries.

Recollect that you must be a seaman to be an officer and that you cannot be a good officer without being a gentleman.

Duty is the great business of a sea officer; all private considerations must give way to it, however painful it may be.

—Admiral Horatio Nelson

Lord Horatio Nelson was one of Britain's greatest naval commanders. He had a long and distinguished career in which he gained a reputation as a master tactician and for great personal bravery. Nelson is a compelling example of someone who has found and embraced their role. At the age of only twelve, Nelson joined the navy as an apprentice working in the lowest naval ranks. However, his aptitude and enthusiasm for his job saw him rapidly rise through the ranks until he was given his own ship and made a captain at only twenty years old. Over the years, Nelson developed a reputation as a very good commander who was daring, bold, and when necessary, willing to disobey orders. He would lose his right arm and the sight in one of his eyes in the fulfillment of his post. Nelson's crowning moment came at the Battle of Trafalgar, where Britain's decisive victory over Napoleon's fleet ended the threat of a French invasion of England. It also cost Nelson his life. Shortly before his death, he was heard to murmur – "*Thank God, I have done my duty.*"

To explore this aspect of your Meta Mindset, reflect upon how clearly you can answer the following questions:

- *What type of person do you need to be, and what role do you need to have to create the life you want as well as succeed in your ambition, mission, and vision?*

- *What is your position with respect to others in your environment/market?*

- *What are the core competencies necessary to be the type of person you need to or to achieve and remain in the necessary position or status?*

META MINDSET AND THE CIRCLE OF SUCCESS

The characteristics of Meta Mindset are crucial for building a sustainable Circle of Success. In summary:

- Personal *passion* comes from connecting fully with your**self** and your deepest **identity** and discovering what brings you enthusiasm and energy. It involves exploring the question, *"What do you really love to do?"*

- *Vision* is a function of your personal passion expressed outwardly to contribute to **customers and the market**. It is the answer to the question, *"What do you want to see improved in the world long term?"*

- The alignment of **team members and employees** working together to reach a vision is a result of communicating and sharing your passion in the form of the *mission* of the project or venture. It is a result of answering the question, *"What is your unique contribution to the vision?"*

- Your passion in the form of your *ambition* to build a successful and sustainable project venture and create value is what motivates **stakeholders and investors** to offer their resources and take the risk to join the venture. It involves being clear about the answer to the question, *"What do you want to achieve concretely?"*

- Your passion for applying your area of excellence in the form of a *role* and building win-win relationships with peers that enrich and leverage resources is what forms the basis for effective **partnerships and alliances**. This requires clarifying, *"Who do you need to be or become to fulfill your mission and ambition?"*

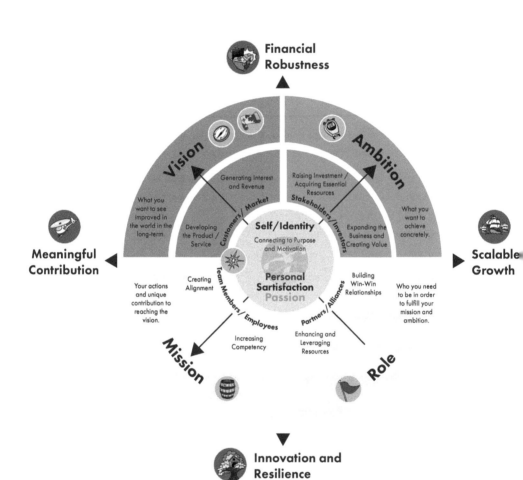

Meta Mindset and the SFM Circle of Success™

SUMMARY: KEY META MINDSETS FOR BUILDING A CIRCLE OF SUCCESS

The Circle of Success is built around your interactions with your customers, team members, stakeholders, and partners. Its purpose is to help you (1) make a meaningful contribution, (2) be more innovative and resilient, (3) grow your business, (4) be more financially profitable, and (5) increase your personal satisfaction.

You can achieve these outcomes through your actions concerning yourself and your customers, team members, stakeholders, and partners. Your ability to succeed in achieving these outcomes is driven by what we call your big picture clarity or Meta Mindset. This level of mindset has five different elements: passionate, visionary, purposeful, ambitious, and accountable.

 Passionate

Your passion is where your energy comes from. Every successful entrepreneur will tell you, "You must have passion for what you're doing." Steve Jobs said, "It's absolutely essential that you have passion because it's difficult to start and run a business, and you have to do it for a sustained period." He said, "In fact, it's so difficult that if you don't have passion, you will give up." Warren Buffet very clearly said, "If you have no passion, you have no energy. And if you have no energy, you have nothing." So, you need to find ways to connect to that passion. Now, that passion is, "What do you love to do? What brings you excitement, energy, enthusiasm, and commitment?" You need ways to keep constantly connecting back to that passion to bring yourself the energy that you're going to need to get through challenging times.

We find our passion through our feelings. It is not an intellectual concept. It is not about rational thinking. It's about coming into your body and really feeling what brings you energy. One way to find your passion is to look back on your history. What things do you love to do? What things would you do no matter what, whether you were paid for it or not? What things make you feel the most alive and the most enthusiastic while you're doing them? What things, when you do them, bring you a very high, committed level of energy?

It is essential to realize that your passion is not the thing you're doing. It's the reason you are doing it and what it brings you. So, if I say, "I have a passion for riding my bicycle," riding the bicycle is not my actual passion. My passion is what I get from riding that bicycle, which might be a sense of freedom or a sense of movement. So, to discover your passion, you must focus on something deeper than the action. Our passion is what is meaningful to us, which could, for example, be harmony, excellence, or health. The five words I use to express my passion are "connection, awakening, creativity, contribution, and inspiration."

Your passion is your first foundation, and that's why we put it in the center of the Circle of Success.

  ### Visionary

Next, we turn that passion into a vision. Passion is something you feel in your body and in the present. You feel it now. Your vision is something you see in the future. So, you go from feeling to seeing. Now, the way we create vision in SFM is to take your passion and begin to look to the future, and even project yourself into the future, and ask, "What do I want to see in the future? What kind of improved world do I want for myself, my family, my community, and especially my customer? What is the world to which I want to belong? What will be transformed? What is going to become better? What will there be less of? What will there be more of?"

Every single successful person and entrepreneur starts from a vision of the possibilities in the future. Your vision is our mental picture of what's possible, of a better world that could be. And so, we take our passion and we turn it into a vision and we express that vision in different ways. We express it as a statement. But we also express it as a metaphor or a symbol. We express it as what's going to be transformed into something else.

What all successful people share is that they are big dreamers. They have a big vision for the future, and they can articulate that vision. They can communicate it. They can passionately own it, and then they can inspire others to join them in working every day to create it. So, that's what your vision is. Where you are going. Your passion gives you energy; your vision gives you direction.

Purposeful

Once you are clear about your passion and vision, you can move to your purpose and mission. Your mission is what you are going to do to reach your vision. What is your unique and special contribution to achieving that vision? Whether it's you as a person, you as a team, or your organization, your mission is the action you must take. So, passion is a feeling and its energy, vision is an image giving direction, and mission relates to the actions taken when you put your energy into action, into movement, to reach your vision.

Your mission is what you're going to do uniquely for your customers. Your mission relates to your product, your project, the tools you're either creating or providing, or the service you're giving. Your mission is where you move into action. Your vision comes from dreaming, while your mission is where you start moving into a realist mindset. You will start to realize your vision through what you do and what you bring to your customers.

Ambitious

The next part of building your Circle of Success and the next area of Meta Mindset is *ambition*. Ambition comes from the desire to achieve concrete results. Passion is not a result; it is energy. Your vision is a big dream. Your mission is an action. Your ambition is what you want to concretely accomplish. This does not mean small objectives; your ambition is your big goals that usually span at least one or two years, sometimes five. Ambition is not abstract; it's measurable. For example, "I want to double the size of my business, I want to have X number of customers, I want to achieve X percent profitability, etc." So, your ambition comes in the form of the achievements you make that are creating the path leading you to your vision. Again, your ambition comes from your desire for achievement and mastery. Every successful person is also ambitious. Not only are they visionary and have passion and energy, but they're also ambitious. They have a strong desire to achieve something concretely in the world.

Accountable

This leads us to the final part of your Circle of Success and your Meta Mindset, which is being clear and accountable with respect to your *role*. The idea of your role is as you put your passion into action through your mission, go toward your vision, and start to achieve your ambition, you will become more. Your role will expand along with your responsibilities. Who you are in the world, your potential, and the impact you make will increase. So, we say you feel your passion, you see your vision, you do your mission, you achieve your ambition, and through achieving, you become. You become something more, something bigger. You have more possibilities and more influence. Your role is not necessarily your deepest identity. In many ways, of course, you remain the same person. Your role is more about the possible expression of that deeper identity and expansion of who you can be in the world.

When you're clear about all the elements of your success mindset, you have the fundamental recipe for success and are ready to start your venture or project or to take it to the next level. You are prepared to live your dream and make a better world through your business.

Assessing Meta Mindset

To assess the above crucial dimensions of Meta Mindset, the Success *MindsetMaps Inventory* uses a system of self-rating. The inventory takes users through a series of statements, including:

- *I know what I really love to do (I know what I am passionate about).*

- *I know what I want to help create in the longer-term future (I am clear about my destination and my longer-term vision).*

- *I am clear about my direction, regardless of whether I know the ultimate destination.*

- *I know my purpose; I know what I stand for and why I am doing what I am doing. I am clear about my mission, and the unique contribution I want to make through my venture.*

- *I am clear about my ambition, i.e., what I want to become and achieve in the next two to five years.*

- *I am clear about my role, i.e., the position I have with respect to others in my market/environment.*

Users then rate the truth of each statement for themselves on a scale of 1–10, where 10 is the truest and 1 is not true at all. Given the user's Meta Goal, i.e., their current focus and the level of rating, the MindsetMap will suggest a tool in relation to that area of Meta Mindset.

If the rating is high (7 or greater), the MindsetMap will suggest a tool to be applied by the user and their coach to help reinforce that area of Meta Mindset so that the user can keep it at a high level.

If the rating is *medium* (4 or greater but less than 7), the MindsetMap will recommend a tool that can be applied by the user and their coach to increase that area of Meta Mindset to a higher level.

If the rating is *low* (less than 4), the MindsetMap will recommend a tool that can be applied by the user and their coach to begin to develop that area of their Meta Mindset with special attention to working with potential obstacles or resistances to that area of mindset.

The Success MindsetMap Inventory stores and presents the user's Meta Mindset ratings in a *Premium Report* that can be shared with a certified MindsetMaps coach. The Premium Report represents the user's Meta Mindset ratings in several forms, as shown in the accompanying illustration, rank ordering the results and pointing out the user's top three strengths.

Meta Mindset Statements	Rating
I know what I really love to do (I know what I am passionate about).	9
I know what I want to help create in the longer term future (I am clear about my destination; and my longer term vision)	8
I am clear about my direction, regardless of whether or not I know the ultimate destination.	8
I know my purpose – I know what I stand for and why I am doing what I am doing. I am clear about my mission – the unique contribution I want to make through my venture.	10
I am clear about my ambition – i.e., what I want to become and achieve in the next two to five years.	9
I am clear about my role – i.e., the position I have with respect to others in my market/environment.	7

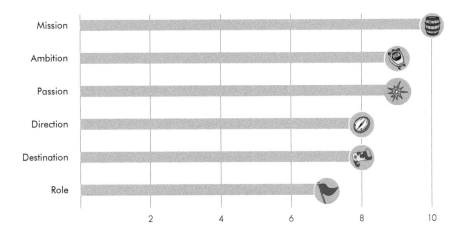

These results are a vital part of the MindsetMaps coaching process, which is illustrated in the application case example in Chapter 5.

SUCCESS MINDSET CASE EXAMPLE: OPRAH WINFREY

The extraordinary success of talk show diva and media mogul Oprah Winfrey provides a compelling illustration of how *mindset matters most.* Claiming that "The greatest discovery of all time is that a person can change their future by merely changing their attitude." Winfrey advises, "If you want your life to be more rewarding, you have to change the way you think."

Born into poverty in rural Mississippi to a teenage single mother and later raised in an inner-city Milwaukee neighborhood, Winfrey was molested during her childhood and early teenage years. She became pregnant at fourteen, and her son was born prematurely and died in infancy. When fired from her first broadcasting job, she was told that she "wasn't fit for TV." Winfrey, however, persisted, boosting a third-rated local talk show to first place. She then launched her own production company, becoming a millionaire by thirty-two and the first black woman billionaire in world history. As of 2022, Winfrey had a net worth of more than 3.5 billion dollars. In addition to her financial success, Winfrey has won eighteen Emmy Awards and a Tony Award and received two Academy Award nominations. She has also been given several humanitarian awards for her extensive philanthropic work and, in 2013, was presented with the Presidential Medal of Freedom.

Winfrey's remarkable journey to success is a testament to the power of mindset. As she points out, "With every experience, you alone are painting your own canvas, thought by thought, choice by choice." She goes on to explain, "Doing the best at this moment puts you in the best place for the next moment." This is the way that you build a path to a successful future, step-by-step.

Key to this mindset is understanding the power of purpose. As Winfrey puts it, "I've come to believe that each of us has a personal calling that's as unique as a fingerprint and that the best way to succeed is to discover what you love and then find a way to offer it to others in the form of service, working hard and allowing the energy of the universe to lead you."

Interestingly, Winfrey's description is precisely what we call a *Next-Generation Entrepreneur;* someone committed to living their dreams and making a better world through their business. This involves building what we call a "Circle of Success."

According to Success MindsetMaps, we build our Circle of Success with the guidance of several key attributes of what we call *Meta Mindset*, namely Passion, Vision, Mission, Ambition, and Role. Not surprisingly, Winfrey's statement about the best way to succeed contains them all, "*to discover what you love* (Passion) *and then find a way to offer it to others* (Vision) *in the form of service* (Mission), *working hard* (Ambition), *and allowing the energy of the universe to lead you* (Role)."

Let's look more deeply at what Oprah Winfrey's journey can teach us about developing the characteristics of mindset necessary to create a thriving Circle of Success.

IDENTITY AND PASSION

Self/Identity
Connecting to Purpose and Motivation

Personal Sartisfaction Passion

At the center of the Circle of Success are your identity and passion. According to the Success MindsetMap, your clarity about your identity and your passion forms the foundation for all the other parts of the circle. If these foundations are vague or uncertain, building a sustainable Circle of Success is not possible. The main focus of the center of the Circle of Success is connecting to purpose and motivation. In the words of Oprah Winfrey, "As you become more clear about who you really are, you'll be better able to decide what is best for you – the first time around."

Passion is *an intense desire or enthusiasm for something*. It has to do with answering questions like:

- *What do I really love to do?*
- *What am I excited about?*
- *What do I find to be interesting and compelling?*
- *What brings me a deep sense of enthusiasm and energy?*

These are crucial to answer in order to reach success. All outstanding performances begin with passion. As Winfrey points out, "Passion is energy," and "Energy is the essence of life. Every day you decide how you're going to use it by knowing what you want and what it takes to reach that goal, and by maintaining focus." To do what is necessary to succeed, Winfrey maintains that it is important to "feel the power that comes from focusing on what excites you."

VISION

Vision involves creating a mental image of what the future could or will be like. It is especially focused on what you want to see improved in the world in the long term. The Meta Mindset characteristic of Vision is knowing what you want to help create in the longer-term future and being clear about your direction, regardless of whether you know the ultimate destination. Your vision emerges as you look to the future through the filter of your passion. As Winfrey asserts, "You have to know what sparks the light in you so that you, in your own way, can illuminate the world."

Vision

What you want to see improved in the world in the long-term.

Every single successful person and successful entrepreneur starts from a vision of the possibilities in the future. General Electric's Jack Welch, heralded by many as one of the greatest corporate leaders of his era, claimed, "Good business leaders create a vision, articulate the vision, passionately own the vision, and relentlessly drive it to completion." Reflecting on how she created her many successful ventures, Winfrey explains, "Before you embark on any quest, you must first articulate your vision. Set your course. It doesn't have to be a public or formal declaration, but it does need to be clear."

Brian Tracy points out in his book *The Psychology of Achievement*, "All successful people, men and women, are big dreamers. They imagine what their future could be, ideal in every respect, and then they work every day toward their distant vision, that goal or purpose." Similarly, Winfrey urges people to dream big and "Create the highest, grandest vision possible for your life."

MISSION

Your actions and unique contribution to reaching the vision.

Once you are clear about your Passion and Vision, you move to your Mission. Your Mission is about service. What is your unique contribution to achieving your vision? It is about moving from dreamer to realist and putting your Passion into action. As Winfrey says, "The key to realizing a dream is to focus not on success but significance – and then even the small steps and little victories along your path will take on greater meaning." She goes on to add, "What I know is, is that if you do work that you love, and the work fulfills you, the rest will come."

Mission relates to the actions taken when you put your Passion and energy into motion to reach your Vision. Clarifying your Mission involves knowing what you stand for and why you are doing what you are doing. It comes from being clear about the unique contribution you want to make. According to Winfrey, "Everyone has a calling. Your real job in life is to figure out, as soon as possible, what that is and who you are meant to be and begin to honor your calling in the best way possible."

AMBITION

The next part of building your Circle of Success and the next key characteristic of a success mindset is *Ambition*. Ambition comes from the drive for growth and mastery. As Winfrey puts it, "The choice to be excellent begins with aligning your thoughts and words with the intention to require more from yourself." Every successful person is ambitious. They have a strong desire to make a concrete difference through their achievements. Steve Jobs famously talked about his aspiration "to put a dent in the universe," claiming that "the only way to be truly satisfied is to do what you believe is great work." Winfrey echoes this when she states, "Unless you choose to do great things, it makes no difference how much you are rewarded or how much you have."

What you want to achieve concretely.

Your Ambition is what you want to concretely achieve. It is not abstract; it's measurable. For example, "I want to double the size of my business. I want to have X number of customers. I want to achieve X percent profitability." So, your Ambition comes in the form of your commitment to actual achievements that are creating the path that is leading you to your Vision. Winfrey advises, "Every time you state what you want or believe, you're the first to hear it. It's a message to both you and others about what you think is possible. Don't put a ceiling on yourself."

ROLE

Who you need to be in order to fulfill your mission and ambition.

Role

You achieve your Ambition, fulfill your Mission, reach your Vision, and express your Passion through your role. *Role* relates to both the professional position you occupy with respect to others and the expected capabilities and behaviors attached to that position. Finding the right role for yourself (and others) is one of the most crucial and sometimes most challenging aspects of building your Circle of Success. Even if you have a clear sense of Passion, Vision, Mission, and Ambition, if you are in a Role that is not aligned with them, you struggle. As mentioned earlier, Winfrey was fired from her first broadcasting job. As she describes it, "Up until then, I'd been a news anchor and reporter. I knew I was not my authentic self. And my bosses certainly made no secret of their feelings. They told me I was the wrong color, the wrong size and that I showed too much emotion."

It wasn't until she was "unceremoniously demoted" to cohost of a third-rated local talk show that Winfrey's true role began to become clear. At the end of the first show, she felt "a sense of knowing resonating within my heart and radiating to the hairs on the back of my neck. My entire body told me this was what I was supposed to do. As a reporter, I'd been exhausted all the time. I really had to drag myself into work. But after one day on this local talk show, I was energized in a way that fueled every cell of my being. There was no doubt that the seeds of what was to give my life meaning and purpose had been planted."

As you achieve through your Role, it will evolve and expand. Who you are in the world and the potential that you have will get bigger. You become something more. You have more possibilities and more influence. Your Role is the channel of expression of your deeper identity and the potential of who you can be in the world. Winfrey herself, for instance, realized at a certain moment that her Role had expanded beyond being "the most successful talk show host of all time," and she left that Role to start her own media network.

Seeking the right Role requires the proper mindset. As Winfrey's experience illustrates, people are most successful in Roles that are "compatible with their personal characteristics and skills." Your success in finding the proper Role is further enhanced by identifying your "area of excellence." However, as Winfrey points out, "Often, we don't even realize who we're meant to be because we're so busy trying to live out someone else's ideas. But other people and their opinions hold no power in defining our destiny." Instead, Winfrey advises, "Find your lane. Make space for the flow to show itself. Follow the natural rhythm of your life, and you will discover a force far greater than your own."

OVERCOMING CHALLENGES AND MOVING FORWARD

Of course, the journey to success is never simple or straightforward. There are many challenges on the way. In the mindset of successful people, however, challenges are something to be embraced, not avoided. Pointing out that "You get to know who you really are in a crisis," Winfrey maintains, "Whatever you fear most has no power – it is your fear that has the power." She contends, "Challenges are gifts that force us to search for a new center of gravity. Don't fight them. Just find a different way to stand."

Sometimes this requires taking time to reflect and making sure you are internally grounded and resourceful and have ways to recharge and balance yourself. As Winfrey points out, "If you neglect to recharge a battery, it dies. And if you run full speed ahead without stopping for water, you lose momentum to finish the race."

Ultimately, Winfrey argues, "You don't become what you want; you become what you believe." She claims clearly that her mindset has been the key to all her success. In addition to building a strong sense of Passion, Vision, Mission, Ambition, and Role, some significant principles she has followed to build her path to success include:

- "Turn your wounds into wisdom."

- "Surround yourself with only people who are going to lift you higher."

- "Always continue the climb. It is possible for you to do whatever you choose, if you first get to know who you are and are willing to work with a power that is greater than yourself to do it."

- "Understand that the right to choose your own path is a sacred privilege. Use it. Dwell in possibility."

06.

MACRO MINDSET–
HABITS OF
SUCCESS

Macro Mindset relates to the mental disciplines and practices required to bring focus to the big picture of your venture's and begin to put it into action. Like lifting barbells, such practices strengthen the mental discipline necessary for sustainable success. These involve such capabilities as managing your energy and focus, seeking honest and frequent feedback, scanning for opportunities, dealing effectively with risks and adversity, and recharging and balancing yourself.

The Macro Mindset of successful entrepreneurs and leaders is made up of the following five habits of success. We have selected quotes from several successful entrepreneurs to help define and clarify the significance and purpose of each practice. Continuing with our metaphor of the journeys taken by the early explorers, we have also created icons related to the resources necessary to successfully complete a major ocean voyage.

1. ENERGIZER

Do what you are passionate about and invest a lot of energy and focus into making what you want happen.

We have chosen the symbol of the *sail* for this aspect of mindset as it indicates that you have the energy and motivation for your venture and are ready to go "full sail" for what you want. This is an essential attribute for beginning or completing any entrepreneurial endeavor.

It's very rewarding when you work on something that you think is going to make a big difference. Yes, it's a little bit harder, but I think the passion one might bring with it brings so much more energy to that that you are more likely to succeed.

Sergey Brin – Google

You have to have an emotional investment in what you are doing. If you don't love what you are doing, failure is pretty much guaranteed. Success is not guaranteed by any means, but failure is much more likely if you don't love what you are doing.

Biz Stone – Twitter

To explore this aspect of your Macro Mindset, reflect upon the following questions:

- *Are you passionate and motivated about what you are doing?*
- *How much time and energy are you investing in achieving what you want with respect to your project or venture? How consistently do you do that?*
- *How focused are you on making sure that your project or venture fulfills its purpose and is progressing the way you want it to?*

2. SEEKER

– Seek feedback and have established ways to get honest and frequent feedback.

We have chosen the symbol of the *telescope* or *spyglass* for this aspect of mindset as it indicates that you have the means to get ongoing and relevant feedback. Getting honest and frequent feedback is an important habit of success to avoid problems and obstacles and make necessary course corrections.

Constantly seek out criticism. A well thought out critique of whatever you are doing is as valuable as gold. And you should seek that from everyone you can, but particularly your friends.

Elon Musk – Tesla, SpaceX

There are a lot of people from whom you can learn a lot. And I think the one piece of advice is don't underestimate anyone you come across, whether they are a blue collar worker waiting for the bus or they are the server or bartender at a restaurant or they are a lower ranking employee. The smartest leaders I've ever seen have always gone around the table and asked for everyone's opinion.

Chris Sacca – Baller Investor

What you really need to do is think, "What is the smallest possible test that I can run for this idea, for this concept, for this theory?" Get it out there and get customers using it, because your customers are going to be the ones to tell you if its really working or not.

Leah Busque – TaskRabbit

To explore this aspect of your Macro Mindset, reflect upon the following questions:

- *How often do you seek feedback with respect to your project or venture?*

- *Do you have a system in place to get regular feedback?*

- *How effective is the feedback you are receiving with respect to your project or venture?*

- *How do you respond to honest feedback regarding your project or venture, even if it is critical?*

3. **SCANNER**

Constantly scan for opportunities and invest time to create them.

 We have chosen the symbol of the *crow's nest* for this aspect of mindset as it indicates that you have the habit in place to consistently scan your horizon for possibilities and "weak signals" that may indicate significant opportunities. This is a key characteristic of all successful entrepreneurs.

One thing I do is question a lot of things. And you can do that in a good way or a bad way. But hopefully, you get people to examine why they are doing something and the way they are thinking.

The worst thing you can end up with is a situation where you get told, "Well, this is the way it's always been." That's the worst ever. That's a non-answer. Instead, ask yourself, "Given everything we have today, is there a way we can make this better?"

Daniel ek – Spotify

So, when we are coming up with ideas, we always ask ourselves, "What kind of new market is this creating?" And then, "What part of my day and what problem is it solving?" And so, I've gone as far as taking an entire catalog of my day from the moment I open my eyes and writing down every single thing that I do, and then asking myself, "Is there something here?"

Kevin Rose – Digg

To explore this aspect of your Macro Mindset, reflect upon the following questions:

- *Do you scan for opportunities on a regular basis? How and how frequently?*

- *How are you making sure that you are also including "weak signals" that may indicate important opportunities.*

- *What are you doing to create opportunities? How much time and energy do you devote to doing that?*

4. RECHARGER

Are internally grounded and resourceful and have ways of recharging and balancing yourself and practice them daily.

We have chosen the symbol of the *hammock* for this aspect of mindset as it indicates that you have the means and the discipline to be able to take care of yourself and not become overly stressed or burned out. Having practices that keep you grounded, balanced, and recharged is an essential property of sustained and healthy success.

I've had to deal with lots of mentally challenging situations, like when my world sailing record attempts failed. That's why I keep fit. If your body is sharp, your brain will be sharp.

I run every day. It keeps me fit, keeps the endorphins going and keeps the brain functioning well. I can definitely achieve twice as much in a day by keeping fit.

Richard Branson – The Virgin Group

If you don't love it, you won't make it through the long period of pain that is inevitable. So make sure that you take care of yourself during the process, make sure you take care of your mental health, your physical health while you are doing it, because it is a long road.

Emmett Shear – Twitch

To explore this aspect of your Macro Mindset, reflect upon the following questions:

- *How internally grounded and resourceful do you feel?*
- *What do you do if you do not feel grounded and resourceful?*
- *What are your practices for recharging and bringing some type of balance?*
- *What do you do daily to ensure that you are recharged and balanced?*

5. PERSISTER

Are aware of risks and potential problems and don't get discouraged or distracted in the face of adversity and negative feedback.

We have chosen the symbol of the *steering wheel* or *helm* for this aspect of mindset as it indicates that you have the tools and resources to remain in control under challenging and changing conditions. Remaining focused and staying the course are two of the most important attributes of successful entrepreneurs. It is necessary to know how to take the helm and steer through stormy waters.

So many things go wrong when you are starting a company.
And people often ask, "What mistakes should you avoid making?"
And my answer to that question is, "Don't even bother to try to avoid
making mistakes because you are going to make tons of mistakes.
The important thing is to learn quickly from whatever mistakes you
make and not giving up. There are things that every single year
of Facebook's existence could have killed us or made it so that it
seemed like moving forward or making any progress just seemed
intractable. But you kind of bounce back and you learn. Nothing is
impossible. You have to just keep running through the walls.

Mark Zuckerberg – Facebook

So just go and do it, try it, learn from it. You will fail at some things.
That's a learning experience that you need so that you can take it on
to the next experience. And don't let people who you may respect,
and who you believe know what they are talking about, don't let
them tell you it can't be done, because often they will tell you it can't
be done, but that 's because they just don't have the courage to try it.

Pierre Omidyar – eBay

Optimism has a place, but I think even more so for the first-time entrepreneur you need to be pragmatically pessimistic. What I mean by that is you need to define all the worst-case scenarios in terms of financial loss, time loss, etc., look at what you will learn if that happens and accept and come to terms with that before you ever start. If you don't do that and you go straight in to battling the world, trying to conquer the world with rose colored glasses on, the first time you hit a major hiccup you are going to become really demoralized and you'll quit.

Tim Ferriss – 4 Hour Work Week

To explore this aspect of your Macro Mindset, reflect upon the following questions:

- *What do you do to stay aware of possible risks and problems with respect to your project or venture?*

- *What tools and resources do you have to help you remain in control under challenging and changing conditions?*

- *What do you do to remain focused and "stay the course" in the face of adversity and negative feedback?*

Macro Mindset and the Circle of Success

Like the key qualities of Meta Mindset, the habits of success supported by Macro Mindset are essential for building a sustainable Circle of Success.

- **Energizer –** Having energy and focus helps you be clear about your *self and identity* and be sure you are connected to your motivation and purpose.

- **Seeker –** Getting frequent and honest feedback is necessary to develop useful and effective products and services for *customers* and to generate interest and revenue.

- **Scanner –** Scanning for opportunities is essential for building win-win relationships with potential *partners* and to enhance and leverage resources.

- **Recharger –** Being grounded and resourceful is important to keep aligned as a *team* and to be able to increase competency without becoming overwhelmed.

- **Persister –** Staying determined and resilient is crucial for establishing credibility with *stakeholders* and acquiring investment and essential resources to grow the business.

Summary – The Importance of Macro Mindset to Building a Circle of Success

Another way of thinking about the habits of success associated with the various Macro Mindsets is the notion of practice. Success of any type requires practice. The term *practice* means "to do or perform often, customarily, or habitually." It is used to refer to an actual performance or application (i.e., "They were ready to carry out in practice what they advocated in principle.") As the great Greek philosopher Aristotle pointed out, "*We are what we repeatedly do. Excellence, then, is not an act, but a habit.*"

Thus, practices can be viewed as repeated or customary activities to install or improve some pattern of behavior that pragmatically serves the achievement of a goal. In building a Circle of Success, they are also an expression of key areas of our Meta Mindset, namely Passion, Vision, Mission, Ambition, and Role.

 Energizer

Energy and focus are clearly connected with the Meta Mindset quality of *Passion*. Passion creates energy and purpose creates focus. That is why the Macro Mindset associated with energy and focus is about repeatedly reconnecting with your passion, motivation, and purpose. This is how you continue to clarify and reinforce the center of our Circle of Success – Self and Identity. This mindset is perhaps best expressed by advice from Martha Graham, one of the most significant founders of modern expressive dance:

> *There is a vitality, a life force, a quickening that is translated through you into action, and because there is only one of you in all time, this expression is unique. If you block it, it will never exist through any other medium and be lost. The world will not have it. It is not yours to determine how good it is; nor how it compares with other expressions. It is your business to keep the channel open.*

Successful people make it their business to "keep their channel open." We refer to the state of having the "channel open" as the *COACH state*. In fact, this state is the foundation of the MindsetMaps coaching process. The letters COACH form an acronym that stands for five key qualities:

Centered in yourself – especially in the "gut" (your belly center)

Open to possibilities, and able to both give and receive

Attentive to what is going on within you and around you

Connected to your passion, motivation, and purpose

Holding whatever is happening from a state of resourcefulness and curiosity

Practicing the COACH state is something we recommend as a daily exercise for every individual and group that we work with. It is a simple but powerful habit to help people maintain energy and focus that can be done in a matter of a few minutes or even seconds, with enough experience.

 Seeker

Leadership guru Ken Blanchard pointed out long ago that "feedback is the breakfast of champions." Years of research on feedback has shown that:

a. Without some kind of relevant feedback, there is no improvement of performance.

b. Progressive gains in proficiency occur in the presence of relevant feedback.

c. Performance is disrupted when relevant feedback is withdrawn.

d. The higher the relative frequency of feedback, the greater the facilitation of performance.

e. The more specific the feedback, the better the performance

The Macro Mindset focus of seeking feedback and having established ways to get honest and frequent feedback is connected to the Meta Mindset quality of *Vision*. As we have pointed out, Vision is about what you want to see more of in the future. Vision sets a long-term goal and direction. Getting high quality and effective feedback is essential to knowing you are moving in the right direction and progressing toward what you want to achieve regarding your products or services and your customers. Frequent and honest feedback from your customers and market is also key to generating interest and revenue.

 Scanner

To succeed, individuals, teams, and companies need to identify new trends quickly in order to take advantage of opportunities. A significant factor in successful innovation is the ability to detect "weak signals" that herald new and previously unmet needs and interests. Attending to and responding to weak signals relating to emerging challenges and changes in the environment is also key to remaining resilient.

In the book *Alpha Leadership*, Robert and his co-authors use the analogy of frogs and bats to illustrate the importance of scanning for opportunities and detecting weak signals. Frogs and bats share the same food source, flying insects, but employ completely different mindsets for catching their prey. Frogs sit on lily pads waiting for the food to come to them. Frogs are also notoriously poor at detecting weak signals. They are only able to detect the most obvious features of flying insects. Unless something is a certain size and shape and moves in a certain way, a frog will fail to recognize it as food. A frog can actually starve to death in a box of flies if they do not move. In contrast, bats use sophisticated sonar systems capable of detecting extremely minute signals to go out and track down their prey with impressive facility. A single brown bat, for example, can catch around 1,200 mosquito-sized insects in one hour. Frogs can only see and react to the most obvious and nearby opportunities; bats proactively seek and listen carefully for subtle signals at a distance.

However, the most significant point of the comparison has to do with the widely differing life spans of these two creatures. Most frogs live an average of about two to five years. Bats, on the other hand, have an average life span of twenty-five to forty years! Thus, the bat has clearly evolved a much longer-term survival strategy.

The Macro Mindset of scanning for opportunities and investing time to create them is most connected with the Meta Mindset of *Role* and the actions of building win-win relationships and enhancing and leveraging resources. We often ask the individuals and teams that we coach whether they are more "frog-like" or "bat-like" in this regard. Frog-like people sit and wait for opportunities to partner and to leverage resources to come to them. They metaphorically subsist on "low hanging fruit." Bat-like individuals and teams are constantly looking for and proposing possibilities. Because they are on the lookout for opportunities, they often find opportunities that others fail to see.

Recharger

If you are not internally grounded and resourceful, it makes it much more difficult to successfully and sustainably take the actions and exert the effort necessary for your project or venture. Thus, it is important to have ways of recharging and balancing yourself and practice them daily. The area of Meta Mindset most linked with Macro Mindset recharging and balancing is that of *Mission*, which is about your actions and contributions to achieving the Vision of your project or venture.

To engage successfully in your mission, you and other team members must be aligned and committed to continually increasing your competencies. Actively pursuing your Mission can involve a tremendous amount of effort, risk and, at times, adversity. That is a key reason why the habits of recharging and balancing are so important. Without them, you and other team members can burn out.

Staying internally grounded and resourceful are skills related to what is known as the inner game. The *inner game* is about mobilizing our inner resources, overcoming self-imposed obstacles, and staying committed to your goals. As every successful athlete, leader, and performer knows, to win the outer game, you must first succeed in the inner game. It is probably self-evident to most of us that if, in your attempt to achieve an outer goal you meet an inner obstacle, it is going to be much more difficult to accomplish that the outer goal. If you meet an outer obstacle with inner resources, you will approach it as a challenge and give your best to succeed

Fundamental to the inner game is our ability to stay in an optimal performance state when confronted with difficult circumstances. During a time of adversity or crisis, you have a choice. Either you find your inner zone of excellence and re-energize yourself by connecting to your Mission and inner resources, or you give in to the challenges and obstacles you face. When you can ground in on your "inner zone," actions flow with a type of effortless excellence. Some indicators that you are focused and in "the zone" are:

- A sense of "humble authority" – self-confidence without arrogance, a feeling of confidence and the absence of anxiety and self-doubt.

- A state of relaxed readiness in the body and focused spaciousness in the mind.

- Performance comes without effort and without having to think about it.

The opposite of this state – feelings of anxiety, lack of confidence, low energy, fear, stress, and mental and emotional paralysis – are responsible for many difficulties and failures. To put it another way, *limitations in people limit their performance, which limits the venture.* That is why habitually engaging your inner game to stay grounded and resourceful, with the help of a coach, is so valuable.

 Persister

A key success factor in any project or venture is being aware of risks and potential problems and yet not getting discouraged or distracted in the face of adversity and negative feedback. This Macro Mindset is especially important when you are seeking to acquire investment and other essential resources, actively endeavoring to grow your business, and working to achieve other concrete objectives. That is why this habit of success is most connected to the Meta Mindset area of *Ambition.*

Regularly making a *risk analysis* is a key expression of this Macro Mindset. The purpose of making a risk analysis is to think through possible risks, plan for probable liabilities, and be confident that your project or venture can survive if significant challenges arise. The important thing is to anticipate and be prepared for the most significant risks. You don't need to consider and address every possible scenario, rather pick the risk categories that are most relevant to your project or venture and be ready to respond with how you would deal with them. To the extent possible, it is important to consider what your response would be to the risks you anticipate.

By showing stakeholders some of the alternatives you've thought through, you will raise both their and your team's confidence that you'll be able to respond creatively and effectively if things start to go amiss.

Another key aspect of this area of Macro Mindset is revisiting and reinforcing belief in the project or venture, in what you are doing, and your capabilities. We pointed out in the introduction that beliefs play a powerful role in mindset. In our MindsetMap coaching process we put significant attention on several key areas of beliefs: (1) that the project or venture is important and worth it, (2) that it is possible to achieve it, (3) that what you are doing will be effective, (4) that you have the capabilities necessary to do what needs to be done, and (5) that you deserve to achieve your ambitions.

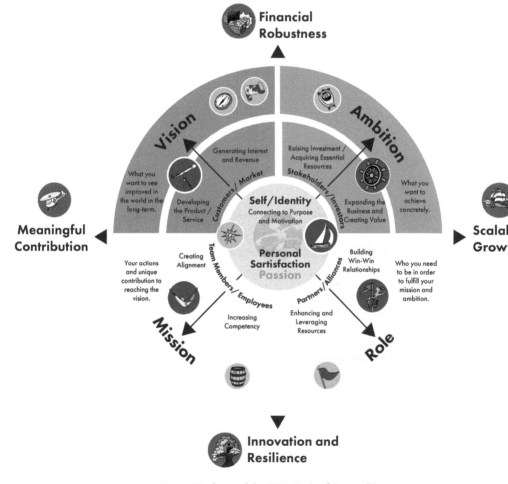

Macro Mindset and the SFM Circle of Success™

Assessing Macro Mindset

Like the assessment of Meta Mindset, the Success MindsetMap Inventory uses a system of self-rating to assess the Macro Mindset habits of success. The inventory takes users through a series of statements, like:

- *I am doing what I am passionate about and invest a lot of energy and focus into making what I want happen.*

- *I seek feedback and have established ways to get honest and frequent feedback.*

- *I am constantly scanning for opportunities and invest time to create them.*

- *I am internally grounded and resourceful and have my ways of recharging and balancing myself and practice that on a daily basis.*

- *I am aware of risks and potential problems and don't get discouraged or distracted in the face of adversity and negative feedback.*

Again, users rate the truth of each statement for themselves on a scale of 1–10, where 10 is the most true for the user and 1 is not true for them at all. And, given the user's Meta Goal and the level of rating, the MindsetMap will suggest a particular tool in relation to that area of Macro Mindset.

If the rating is *high* (7 or greater), the MindsetMap will suggest a tool to be applied by the user and their coach to help reinforce that Macro Mindset habit of success so that the user can keep it at a high level.

If the rating is *medium* (less than 7 but 4 or greater), then the MindsetMap will recommend a tool that can be applied by the user and their coach to increase that Macro Mindset habit of success to a higher level.

If the rating is *low* (less than 4), the MindsetMap will recommend a tool that can be applied by the user and their coach to begin to develop that Macro Mindset habit of success with a special attention to working with potential obstacles or resistances to area of mindset.

As with the Meta Mindset distinctions, the SMI stores and presents the user's Macro Mindset ratings in a Premium Report that can be shared with a certified MindsetMap coach. The Premium Report represents the user's Macro Mindset ratings in several forms, as shown in the accompanying illustration, rank ordering the results and pointing out the user's top three strengths.

Macro Mindset Statements	Rating
I am doing what I am passionate about and invest a lot of energy and focus into making what I want happen.	8
I seek feedback and have established ways to get honest and frequent feedback.	3
I am constantly scanning for opportunities and invest time to create them.	9
I am internally grounded and resourceful and have my ways of recharging and balancing myself and practice that on a daily basis.	6
I am aware of risks and potential problems and don't get discouraged or distracted in the face of adversity and negative feedback.	8

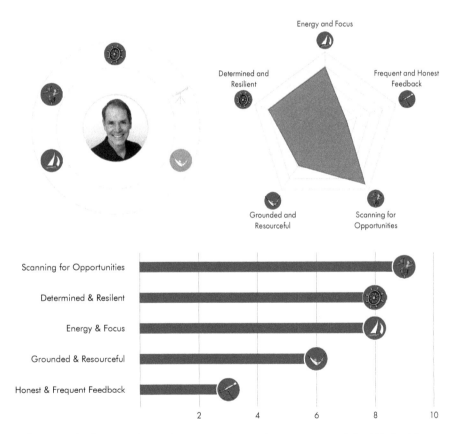

Once again, these results are incorporated as an important part of the MindsetMaps coaching process, which is illustrated in the application case example in Chapter 11.

SUCCESS MINDSET CASE EXAMPLE: KATALIN KARIKÓ

Katalin Karikó, a Hungarian born researcher, has an amazing story. She was very close to getting the Nobel Prize in 2021, but perhaps as a typical turn of her life, she didn't collect the top recognition in the scientific world (yet). She and her close colleague professor Weissman were awarded a $3 million Breakthrough Prize in Life Sciences for their work on modifying the genetic molecule RNA to avoid triggering a harmful immune response. The Breakthrough Prize was founded by Sergey Brin, Priscilla Chan, Mark Zuckerberg, Yuri and Julia Milner, and Anne Wojcicki, to honor groundbreaking discoveries in fundamental physics, life sciences, and mathematics. Karikó has also received the Vilcek Prize for Excellence in Biotechnology, a $100,000 award that recognizes the extraordinary contributions immigrants make to society and culture.

That's where her path has led today, but it didn't start that way. Her discovery of using messenger RNA to treat disease may have become a multi-billion idea that will probably be ultimately responsible for ending the Covid 19 pandemic, but not before it was ignored, missed, and ridiculed. Here is what Angela Merkel, another iconic female public figure, had to say about Karikó's life path:

> The fact that Katalin Karikó sat on the stage today is, of course, more than a symbol. I read your life story with great enthusiasm. We finished our studies at roughly the same time – you in Hungary and I in the GDR (East Germany). Then, you spent an entire life researching something with your finding receiving little recognition at times. It was even sometimes said, "That will probably lead to nothing." You persevered along winding paths and ultimately, we were able to use the thirty years of preparatory work done by you and many others to develop one type of vaccine very quickly. That's an impressive biography.

And indeed, Kati's life (as she is known to her colleagues) was full of rejection and doubt before achieving amazing success and making such a significant and meaningful contribution. In the following case study, we intend to share her story and show the connections between her achievement and her mindset. We will pay specific attention to introducing the qualities of Macro Mindset in her life story, while also attending the other two key levels, Meta and Micro Mindset.

KATALIN KARIKÓ'S META MINDSET

As introduced earlier in this book, Meta Mindset has to do with your clarity and sense of journey. Sometimes, we like to refer to Meta Mindset as "daylight," as it is about your sense-making ability, the mental space to create a story of who you are and why you do what you do. Daylight serves as our dashboard, indicating our direction and providing a compelling vision and sense of purpose and mission. It provides the necessary clarity and visibility of daylight to set our longer-term goals and desires. The key starting point of our Meta Mindset is finding joy and flow in an activity, which often becomes the igniter of our future trajectory both professionally and personally.

Kati was born on January 17, 1955, in the small village of Kisujszallas in Hungary. Her father was a butcher, so she was exposed to a version of "biology" from early age. There was no refrigerator or television in the little house where they lived.

"My mum was an accountant, while my father was a butcher. I knew how to make sausage as a child." What she also knew was that she was passionate about animals and nature, and she loved helping her mom make soap from baking soda and hot water and starting to understand the chemistry behind it.

Like so many people who have achieved extraordinary outcomes, her "daylight" came on quickly and she had a vision from an early age to become a scientist. The way she puts it, "But I was ... very curious and had an amazing teacher who encouraged me a lot." Finding a mentor is a way of seeking feedback and establishing a safe way to get honest and frequent feedback from someone who can do that constructively and with care. We have found that to be one of the fundamental success habits connected with Macro Mindset.

Mindset works by filling in the gaps. You may not be able to see your destination in the future yet, but you can sense your direction. Like Kati said, "When I was sixteen-years-old, all the children were asked what they wanted to be, and I said I would be a scientist. Back then, ten thousand people lived in my small town, so I had never seen a scientist. I didn't really know what a scientist did either, that was just my wish at the time." By connecting her passion to a purpose, she soon developed the very clear sense of direction that has eventually led her to earn her Ph.D. at the University of Szeged and became a postdoctoral fellow at the Biological Research Center.

To succeed, one needs a well-balanced Meta Mindset. At this point in her career, Kati was at the very beginning of defining her exact ambition and role in making that happen. In her own words "The bench is there, the science is good," as she remembered in a recent interview in the NYT "Who cares?" (about the rest...). There was no need to care about a specific destination for a while. In retrospect, she says that "Success to me was decades of working in the laboratory, solving problems. That is what gives me pleasure and excitement every day. The joy of a scientist, to me, is trying to understand the secrets of life, and hoping that one day those secrets can be useful to somebody." This is a very pure way of expressing what the Meta Mindset area of Passion is all about.

This was also time when she became fascinated with the messenger RNA, the genetic script that carries DNA instructions to cells' protein-making engine. This was the first shift that focused her vision on a more specific destination. Destination is a clearer idea of where you would like to get to in terms of results, and how the world will change if you succeed. Kati's vision was that somehow mRNA could play a pivotal role in the therapy of various diseases.

However, when your destination becomes clearer, typically many obstacles occur. These obstacles tend to come from both inside our mind and the external world, which was not initially very receptive of Kati's grand vision. "When your idea goes against the conventional wisdom that makes sense to the star chamber, it is very hard to break out," said Dr. David Langer, a neurosurgeon colleague.

KATALIN KARIKÓ'S MACRO MINDSET

This is where the second level of mindset, Macro Mindset, comes in to play a pivotal role. We sometimes like to refer to it as your "Starlight," which relates to the focus you apply to long-term desires and goals. Starlight works like the stars in the sky. If you feel lost, you can look up, and they help you find your way. We find that the starlight comes from a combination of several activities. These activities include establishing focus on what we have called "Meta Goals." Meta Goals enable you to prioritize the multiple courses of action available to you. Kati chose "making a meaningful contribution" as her Meta Goal. Our Macro Mindset allows us to keep going even if things get tough, and this was very true for her.

How can you tell someone has a strong Macro Mindset? First, you will likely notice that they have observable habits that create a sustainable path to their long-term goals. These include practices of recharging, getting high-quality feedback, reframing criticism, and recharging and balancing in an ongoing manner. In the next part of this case example, we will review Kati's key Macro Mindset habits and qualities and the way they showed up in her journey to success.

 Be internally grounded and resourceful and have ways of recharging and balancing and practice them daily. This element of the Macro Mindset is about the quality of *self-care*.

Interestingly Kati's balancing and recharging came from her family. She is adamant that "women do not need to choose between having a child or having a career." Female scientists and professionals frequently face the dilemma of having to balance being a mother and a professional. Kati has always believed that a woman should not have to choose between her mission as a scientist and her passion as a mother and wife. The key is to find the right type of partner that can support the mission. For her, it was her husband Bela Francia, who was always extremely supportive of Kati's vision and mission. As Kati explains:

> *There is no reason why women should make sacrifices to serve someone. My husband understands and respects the things that are important to me and supports me the same way that I support him. Setting everything aside to put someone first or giving up a career to prioritize your children is simply not a reason to give up.*

 Constantly scan for opportunities and invest time to create them. This element of the Macro Mindset is about the quality of *curiosity*.

Kati is from a small country where there was not enough funding available for her research. Constantly scanning for opportunities is a key life skill that relates to our Macro Mindset. It is about developing the habit of climbing up to the crow's nest and using our metaphorical binoculars to scan the horizon. Like many other scientists, Kati was faced with the choice to stop and do something that was not connected to her passion and mission or to continue at the price of having to leave her home country. In 1985, when she was already married to her husband Bela and had a young daughter, Susan, they decided to leave Hungary to continue to pursue Kati's dream.

Seek feedback and have established ways to get honest and frequent feedback. This element of the Macro Mindset is about the quality of *openness*.

As Kati put it in an award acceptance speech, "Follow your dreams and don't hesitate to learn anything from anyone." As she explains:

> *You can learn from everyone. My daughter, when she was seven-years-old, came home and wrote a letter to her teacher to thank her for the year she had just finished, 'I thank you because we have learned so much,' she wrote. At that time, I was thirty-five years old and had never written a letter to my teachers. I started writing immediately. So, I say to you, don't hesitate to learn anything from anyone, even from a seven-year-old girl, and, above all, tell those who made you understand your value and how important it was for you.*

Be aware of risks and potential problems and don't get discouraged or distracted in the face of adversity and negative feedback. This element of the Macro Mindset is about the qualities of *determination and resilience*.

After scanning the horizon and looking for scholarships and positions all over the world, Kati accepted an offer from Temple University in Philadelphia for a postdoctoral fellowship. It was time to be innovative and resilient. Kati and Bela decided to give up everything and buy a one-way ticket to the USA where they didn't know anyone. They were not allowed to take more than $100 out of the country but they sold their Russian-made car, a Lada, and sewed the money they got for it into their daughter's teddy bear. Such is the power of a strong Macro Mindset at crucial decision points.

Do what you are passionate about and invest a lot of energy and focus into making what you want happen. This element of Macro Mindset is about the quality of *perseverance*.

Dr. Anthony Fauci, director of the National Institute of Allergy and Infectious Diseases, said of Kati and her work, "She was, in a positive sense, kind of obsessed with the concept of messenger RNA." As Kati puts it, "With my colleagues, we worked for years to find this technology. Sometimes, it seemed like science fiction. But we knew that if the result of our work saved the life of even one person, then we had done it. Today, it's a relief to know that these vaccines have saved so many lives and protected so many people from COVID-19."

KATALIN KARIKÓ'S LONG JOURNEY TO SUCCESS

As we continue to track Kati's journey to success, we see the importance and power of her Macro Mindset habits of success. For example, the years she spent in the lab of Temple University could often be frustrating. She explains, "It happened that the experiments didn't work out and that disappointed me a lot. In those moments, I would always read a sentence by Leonardo Da Vinci that said, 'experience does not fail, but only our judgments fail, promising her things that are not in her power.'"

In 1989, Kati joined the University of Pennsylvania's School of Medicine as a research assistant professor. This position does not have much opportunity for professional advancement as it doesn't lead to tenure and requires ongoing grant money to cover the salary. This is where habit of scanning for opportunities became invaluable. As Kati describes:

> When I lived in the US, I saw my colleagues publish in journals much more important than those in which I published. This is why I say to you look at your colleagues, because one day you will need them, you will need their work. Follow them, study what they do, and they will help you.

In that spirit she began working with Dr. Elliot Barnathan, a cardiologist who was also interested in how mRNA could be inserted into cells to induce them to make new proteins. "Most people laughed at us," Dr. Barnathan said. And eventually, as grant money wasn't coming in, Dr. Barnathan left to accept a position with a biotech firm.

The next stakeholder who supported Kati was Dr. Langer, a professor at UPENN. Dr. Langer convinced the neurosurgery department to give Kati's research a chance. Dr. Langer remembers that Kati's mindset was quite different from other scientists he had worked with before. "There's a tendency when scientists are looking at data to try to validate their own idea," he points out. "The best scientists try to prove themselves wrong. Kati's genius was a willingness to accept failure and keep trying, and her ability to answer questions people were not smart enough to ask." We believe this is another testament to her strong Macro Mindset, especially the habit of seeking frequent and honest feedback combined with staying determined and resilient.

At that time, they were hoping to use mRNA to treat patients who developed blood clots following brain surgery. Shortly after, Dr. Langer left the university, and the department chairman was leaving as well. Kati was looking for another lab to join and went through many difficult experiences. "Every night, I was working: grant, grant, grant," she recalled, "And it came back always no, no, no." However, as she said in another interview, her mindset allowed her to bounce back many times: "When I am knocked down, I know how to pick myself up." And the way she did that was simply by reminding herself how much she loved what she was doing and envisioning the difference it could make for others. In her words, "I always enjoyed working... I imagined all of the diseases I could treat." This illustrates the importance and power of the Macro Mindset habit of energy and focus.

Then came 1995, which was a particularly hard year for Kati. She was losing her balance and it showed up in her health. That year, she had cancer scare while her husband Bela was stranded in Hungary dealing with a visa issue. The University of Pennsylvania had just demoted her and no grant money coming was coming in. The support for her to continue was just not there. "I thought of going somewhere else, or doing something else," she says. However, her Macro Mindset habit of continually scanning for opportunities and looking for potential collaborators carried her through.

As fate would have it, in a random meeting with Dr. Drew Weissman in the copy room at the university, some words came to her mouth that eventually changed her whole trajectory. "I said, 'I am an RNA scientist. I can make anything with mRNA,'" she recalls. In that conversation, they discovered that they shared a passion and mission as they were both fascinated by mRNA and its potential use in therapy. Subsequently, they decided to initiate a long and eventful research process together.

The path was far from smooth and they hit many roadblocks. One big problem they needed to solve was that RNA often caused an immune system overreaction. Finally, in 2005, they published their ground-breaking finding, that when mRNA is altered and then delivered into the body it can initiate a protective immune response. Their idea was that this way, you could turn cells into factories that could temporarily produce proteins that would stimulate the body's immune system to attack a specific pathogen while also minimizing a harmful inflammatory response.

Their message at the time was largely ignored. They expected the phone to be ringing constantly after publishing their article, but nobody called. Despite the frustration, and driven by their shared passion, vision, and mission, Kati and Dr. Weissman decided to launch their own company called RNARx, with the aim of focusing on mRNA therapeutics. The company wasn't succeeding, and their funding ran out, but the pair did not give up. Buoyed by their passion and purpose, they continued bringing energy and focus to their research.

THE BREAKTHROUGH

They continued to publish about their groundbreaking discovery and finally, they managed to catch the attention of Moderna of USA and the German company BioNTech. Eventually, both companies licensed their patents. In 2013, BioNTech hired Kati and the company eventually entered a partnership with Pfizer, when the Covid-19 pandemic hit the world. The way she tells the story, when she found out that the Pfizer-BioNTech trials of an mRNA vaccine for Covid-19 had proved successful, she ate an entire box of Goobers chocolate covered peanuts by herself. She was vaccinated on December 18, 2020, at the University of Pennsylvania.

Katalin Karikó's life is testament to finding one's passion and then pursuing it every single day. Many of us know what we are passionate about, but we are not good Self-Motivators on a daily basis. As Kati says, "We spend most of our lives working and it is important that we like it." We also need to learn to manage stress to stay grounded and resourceful. As Kati explains, "I remember when I was in high school, and my teacher gave us a book on stress. That book helped me stay on the path I was on without worrying about what it would be like. It's important that you learn to turn bad stress into good stress."

In the end, when the vaccine worked, it felt like "redemption," Kati told the *Daily Telegraph*. Many scientists never make it to that point. We strongly believe the difference that made the difference for her was her mindset. As Kati claims, "I tried to imagine: Everything is here, and I just have to do better experiments." And that is exactly what she did.

MICRO MINDSET –
ONGOING PRIORITIES

As we have established, our *Micro Mindset* produces and guides the specific actions necessary to build a successful and sustainable project venture. The different aspects of Micro Mindset determine our ongoing priorities. The Micro Mindset of successful entrepreneurs and business leaders is defined with respect to the following nine critical practices which support specific parts of building a Circle of Success:

- The **SelfMotivator** mindset supports our sense of *self and identity* at the center of the Circle of Success by consistently bringing our attention to our purpose and motivation.

- The **ProductCreator** and **MarketMaker** mindsets help to *satisfy customers* and *grow our market* by bringing focus to developing our products and services and generating interest and revenue.

- The **TeamMaker** and **CompetenceBuilder** mindsets support *team members* or *employees* by creating alignment and increasing competency.

- The **FinanSourcerer** and **VentureBuilder** mindsets are oriented towards *stakeholders* and *investors* with the focus on raising investment and acquiring essential resources needed to grow the business and create value.

- The **MatchMaker** and **ReSourcerer** mindsets help to identify and grow *partnerships* and *alliances* by putting attention on building win-win relationships and enhancing and leveraging resources.

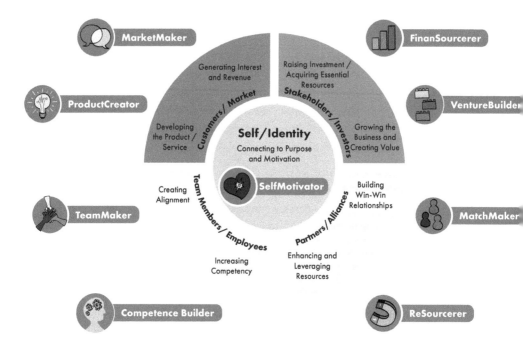

As with the Meta and Macro Mindset, we have selected quotes from several successful entrepreneurs who we have modeled to help define and clarify the significance and purpose of each Micro Mindset.

1. SELFMOTIVATOR:

Setting aside the time to explore and reconnect with what you love to do, what is important to you, and what you are good at doing, i.e., your passion, your sense of purpose, and your excellence.

The focus of the SelfMotivator mindset is to keep an ongoing connection to your purpose, passion, and motivation to live true to yourself and your identity.

I think people who look for great ideas to make money aren't nearly as successful as those who say, "Okay, what do I really love to do? What am I excited about? What do I know something about? What is interesting and compelling?

Michael Dell – Dell

Do something you're very passionate about. And don't try to chase what is kind of the "hot passion of the day."

Jeff Bezos – Amazon.com

To explore this aspect of your Micro Mindset, reflect upon the following questions:

- *Do you set aside time to explore and connect with what you love and why you are doing what you are doing with regard to your project or venture?*

- *Do you feel like you are living true to yourself and your identity with respect to your project or venture?*

- *How strongly is your project or venture connected to what is important to you and what you are good at?*

2. MARKETMAKER:
Creating opportunities for ongoing dialog with customers and prospects.

The focus of the *MarketMaker* mindset is to open and maintain dialog with multiple customers and customer representatives to generate interest and revenue.

It is not just about doing focused groups. It is not just about double-checking your vision. It is really about his concept of testing our ideas rigorously throughout the product development process; throughout the marketing process even as we scale up.

Eric Ries – The Lean Startup

Most startups that fail do it ultimately because they did not make something that people wanted. They made something that they thought people would want, but they were either in denial about whether it was actually any good or somebody else came along and made something that people wanted even more.

Paul Graham – Y Combinator

To explore this aspect of your Micro Mindset, reflect upon the following questions:

- *How frequently do you set aside time for ongoing dialog with customers or prospects for your project or venture?*
- *How open are you to dialog with different types of customers and customer representatives?*
- *How certain are you that your project or venture is providing a product or service that people really want?*

3. PRODUCTCREATOR:

Brainstorming, generating and implementing products, solutions and services that anticipate and fulfill customer needs.

The *ProductCreator* mindset aims to anticipate and fulfill customer needs and desires by developing innovative and empowering solutions (products and services).

> *One way to conceptualize what makes a good project is that good engineering is part of it, good design is part of it, but really one way that I think about it at least is maximizing the probability that someone shows up at the front door of your store or your website or whatever it is and ends up with a solved problem.*
>
> **Drew Houston** – DropBox

> *What this all comes down to is doing something exceptional for your users. Whether its in community, whether its in connection or whether it in design. This is our big advantage as a start up; that we can actually get away with doing that. We can make this the core part of why we are doing business.*
>
> **Alexis Ohanian** – Reddit, Hipmunk

To explore this aspect of your Micro Mindset, reflect upon the following questions:

- *How much time are you devoting to developing the product or service associated with your project or venture?*

- *What are the customer needs or problems that the products or services provided by your project or venture address, fulfill, or solve? How effectively do they fulfill or resolve those needs or problems?*

- *How innovative and up-to-date (with respect to developing technologies and other resources) are the products and services provided by your project or venture?*

4. TEAMMAKER:

Attracting and providing direction and support to team members and encouraging team cooperation.

The emphasis of the *TeamMaker* mindset is to attract and give direction to people who support the mission of the venture (its products and services) by fostering synergy, complementarity, and alignment.

The hardest thing is to start. You have all these ideas and everyone has an idea, but its really about executing the idea and building the idea and attracting other people to help you work on the idea. That is the biggest challenge. But the way to begin is to get the idea out of your head, draw it out, talk about it, program it if you are a programmer or make it if you building something.

Jack Dorsey – Twitter, Square

You don't have to be the best, but you have to be "dangerous." You have to learn just enough to be dangerous to build an idea, concept it and show it to the world. And then it turns out there are lots of other people, including all 170 employees who work at Instagram who are much better at doing all that stuff than I am. But you need to find people that will be drawn to the idea that you build, and then they end up taking it and making it even better.

Kevin Systrom – Instagram

To explore this aspect of your Micro Mindset, reflect upon the following questions:

- *How much time are you devoting to attracting new team members or giving direction and focus to existing team members?*

- *What are you doing to foster synergy, complementarity, and alignment among your team members?*

- *Why would somebody be interested in and willing to be a member of your team?*

- *Are you confident that your team will take the products or services associated with your project or venture and make them better?*

5. COMPETENCEBUILDER:

Encouraging and providing opportunities for team members to learn and grow.

The primary attention of the *CompetenceBuilder* mindset is on providing opportunities and resources necessary for team members to grow and to increase competency.

I often half-jokingly say to a lot of people that my job is basically to be the assistant for the rest of the company. My job is to make sure that you have everything that you need to "kick ass." If you don't have that then let me know, because I am not doing my job.

Andrew Ljung – Soundcloud

I think you should be spending your money on teaching and on sharing. So that might mean hiring a writer or two perhaps instead of a marketing person. And start writing and start getting people to listen to what you are saying. And you can't talk about yourself all the time, because no one is going to come back for that. Talk about things that are relevant for your industry or ideas that you have, and start building up an audience.

Jason Fried – Basecamp

To explore this aspect of your Micro Mindset, reflect upon the following questions:

- *How much of your time do you invest in providing opportunities and resources necessary for your team members to grow and increase their competencies?*

- *Which competencies are the most important for your team members to strengthen?*

- *In what ways do you encourage your team members to learn and grow? What support do you provide them to do that?*

6. FINANSOURCERER:

Identifying potential investors and providers of other essential resources and creatively getting their interest and commitment to support your venture.

The priority of the *FinanSourcerer* mindset is to identify sources of funds and other essential resources (stakeholders and investors) and creatively connect them to the ambitions and strengths of the venture.

But understand that naturally no one is interested in your ideas. The world could care less. And you have to persuade them and you have to show that you are the one person out there that can do it.

Robert Greene – 'Mastery'

So when we see a kid with a lemonade stand its different than when we see a vending machine selling lemonade; even if it is exactly the same product. Because the story around it is what people are paying for. So when I meet small business people, all I ask them is, not what's their balance sheet, but what's their story. Why should I pick you? Why should I care about what you are doing? And if you start giving me all this inside baseball statistics about why you are 2% better than some other competitor I am already glazed over because that's not part of the way I see the world.

Seth Godin – Tribes

For somebody aspiring to take things to the next level or even surpass their wildest dreams, there is always going to be an element of luck. But I think even more important is putting yourself in a business that can be ubiquitous; that really doesn't have limits. There is always going to be a grind to it, but if it can't be something you can visualize every business using or every consumer using, it is going to be tough to scale up to be big enough or to have the perceived value.

Mark Cuban – Cyber Dust

To explore this aspect of your Micro Mindset, reflect upon the following questions:

- *How much time are you currently spending on identifying and pitching to potential investors and providers of other essential resources and support for your project or venture?*
- *Who are your main stakeholders and what types of resources are they providing to support your project or venture?*
- *Why would a potential stakeholder want to invest in, support, or provide resources for your project or venture? What value are you creating for potential stakeholders?*

7. VENTUREBUILDER:

Creating and developing a sustainable infrastructure and a path for growth and scalability of your venture.

The *VentureBuilder* mindset concentrates on establishing a sustainable infrastructure and a path to growth and scalability for the venture to create value for investors and other stakeholders.

*Don't think about "how do I get big really fast?"
That will happen if you build something super meaningful and super important. So don't think about "What's the quickest way to success?" Think about "What's the best way to build something important that the world really needs?"*

Danae Ringelmann – Indiegogo

Often times the best methodology is to start with the perfect experience of just one person, get that right and then figure out how to scale something great; instead of scaling something not so great and then trying to improve it. That's really hard to do.

Brian Chesky – Airbnb

There is almost this expectation that you have to have in your mind this sort of "I am going to change the world or make a dent in the universe" kind of ambition. But its actually okay early on to just kind of solve small problems in layers until you actually have the capacity to do that.

Anthony Casalena – Squarespace

To explore this aspect of your Micro Mindset, reflect upon the following questions:

- *What infrastructure is necessary to grow/ scale your project or venture? How will that create value for your investors or stakeholders?*

- *What is the path by which you intend to grow/ scale your project or venture?*

- *How much of your time and available resources are you devoting to creating the infrastructure and path needed to grow/ scale your project or venture?*

8. MATCHMAKER:

Seeking and establishing win-win relationships with potential partners and allies who resonate with your values and vision.

The focus of the *MatchMaker* mindset is to seek other ventures (partners/ alliances) that share common visions and values and complement one another's roles and strengths (through sharing, combining, or exchanging) to build win-win relationships.

You should find a great partner, no matter what it is that you are doing. And you should look for someone who has very high intelligence, very high energy and very high integrity. You need all three of those and you can't compromise on any one of them. Otherwise, you will end up with someone who is not smart, which does you no good. Or someone who is not hardworking which also does you no good. Or the worse case is you end up with a smart hardworking crook who winds up working against your interests. And integrity is something that takes a lot of time spent with someone to figure out.

Kamal Ravikant – AngelList

The most important thing when you are working with people early on is that you guys line up what your goals are. That sounds really basic. But you can want to run a small business that makes money and you don't have to go to an office every day. Or you can want to build a huge company. You can want to build Google. But I think you have to be really aligned on that.

Ben Silbermann – Pinterest

To explore this aspect of your Micro Mindset, reflect upon the following questions:

- *How many partnerships or alliances do you have that support your project or venture?*

- *How much time do you spend looking for potential partnerships or alliances?*

- *What would be the benefits (wins) to potential partners or allies if they share, combine, or exchange with the products or services associated with your project or venture?*

- *What would be the qualities or characteristics of a good partner for your project or venture? What vision, values, strengths, role, etc.?*

9. RESOURCERER:

Identifying and leveraging synergies between what you are doing and the products, services, or competencies of other ventures

The primary concerns of the *Resourcerer* mindset are to recognize, explore, and implement significant synergies with the products, services, and competencies, etc., of other complementary ventures (partners/ alliances) to enrich and leverage resources.

The most important thing is the individual – whether or not you feel the individual is capable of doing the idea. There are many, many people who have similar ideas and great ideas . . . it's just whether they can actually deliver that idea. So try to work out whether that person will put in all the hours needed, whether they can motivate people. A company is simply a group of people and you want to be actually sure that the person who is coming to you with the idea is somebody that you feel can deliver, and everything else flows from that.

Richard Branson – The Virgin Group

If you are not utilizing an online community then you are at a disadvantage to those who are. You can be asking an online community if they have any ideas or if they have any advice for what you are working on. Not only will you hear from people who are passionate about the subject, but you will be hearing from people all around the world, each with their own experiences and stories who can help you.

Alan Schaaf – Imgur

To explore this aspect of your Micro Mindset, reflect upon the following questions:

- *What potential synergies do the products or services provided by your project or venture have with potential partners or allies?*

- *How could what you are providing through your project or venture enhance or leverage other products or services?*

- *In what ways could the products or services of your project or venture complement those of others? What do you provide that could increase the value of what others are doing?*

Micro Mindset and Meta Goals

As we pointed out earlier, Micro Mindsets are the sources of the key actions defined by the SFM™ Circle of Success. Thus, competence with these mindsets is essential to concretely achieve the outcomes associated with the Circle of Success.

For instance:

- The *ProductCreator* and *TeamMaker* mindsets are essential for making a **meaningful contribution**.

- The *CompetenceBuilder* and *Resourcerer* mindsets are necessary to produce **innovation and resilience**.

- The *MatchMaker* and *VentureBuilder* mindsets are what make it possible to achieve **scalable growth**.

- The *MarketMaker* and *FinanSourcer* mindsets are required to attain **financial robustness**.

- The *SelfMotivator* mindset is the foundation for achieving **personal satisfaction**.

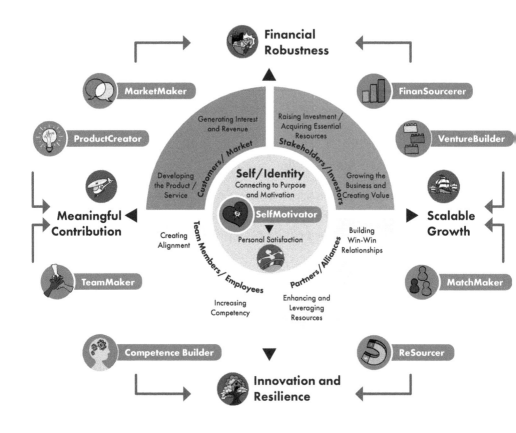

Micro Mindset and the SFM Circle of Success™

Assessing Micro Mindset

As with Meta and Macro Mindsets , you are frequently more competent and comfortable with some of the Micro Mindsets than others. Thus, to build your Circle of Success, you need to either develop some of these mindsets more fully or partner with others who are more naturally inclined to the mindsets you lack to complement your areas of weaknesses.

The MindsetMap Inventory measures Micro Mindset competencies along three dimensions, (1) "I enjoy it," (2) "I am good at it," and (3) "I spend time doing it." The combination of these three determines your "zone of competence," ranging from "waste of time" or "hobby" to "excellence" and "genius."

- If someone enjoys an activity, is good at it, and spends time doing it, this is an area of **excellence** for that person. If that activity is connected to their *passion*, *mission* and *ambition*, it is a potential area of **genius**. That could, however, be an asset or a limitation depending upon whether it is the most important thing for that person to be doing to reach their current focus for their project or venture.

Excellence

- If someone enjoys an activity and is good at it but doesn't spend time doing it, then it is an **untapped excellence**. It means they are probably giving priority to other actions. In this case, the main question is whether it is something they should be spending time with to reach the current focus of their project or venture.

Untapped Excellence

- If someone enjoys an activity and spends time doing it but is not good at it then it is probably more of a **hobby**. It is likely that it is a source of some frustration for them. It is something that would be good for them to get some training or coaching with.

Hobby

- If someone is good at an activity and spends time doing it but does not enjoy it, it likely an area of **competence** that they experience as something necessary but as potentially tedious and boring. It would be useful to explore ways to increase their motivation. It can be helpful, for instance, to spend time with and model someone who genuinely enjoys doing it.

Competence

- If someone enjoys an activity but is not good at it and doesn't spend time doing it then it is most likely just an **interest**. Even though they get pleasure from it, it probably does not add much value when they do. It is definitely something that the person will want to invest the time to learn more about and improve upon, depending upon their goals for their project or venture.

Interest

- If someone spends time doing an activity but does not enjoy it and is not good at it then it is currently an area of **incompetence**. It is likely that the person frequently feels overwhelmed and finds they are "spinning their wheels" or wasting their time, even if they think it is something that is important for them to do. It is clearly an area that they will want to get support developing both their capability and motivation for.

Incompetence

- If someone is good at an activity but neither likes it nor spends time doing it then it is an **untapped competence.** It is clearly an issue of motivation rather than one of competency or priority. It would be useful for them to spend some time better understanding the reasons why it is important and exploring how they might increase their interest and pleasure in doing it.

Untapped Competence

- If someone does not enjoy an activity, is not good at it, and does not spend time doing it then it is currently a **waste of time** for them. It is an obvious area for development, as it is likely that they will need some serious support to develop their motivation and capability in that area, or find a good partner they can trust who has competence in that activity.

Waste of Time

To achieve certain Meta Goals, a person will often need to reach at least a level of excellence in one of the relevant Micro Mindsets. Being competent with that area of Micro Mindset is important, but frequently not enough. If you are good at something and spend time doing it, but don't enjoy it, you are likely to give up or burn out when the situation becomes challenging.

In some cases and contexts, successfully and sustainably achieving a Meta Goal may require a level of genius – where an excellence is connected to the user's Passion, Vision, and Ambition. This ensures that the excellence supports and is supported by the big picture clarity related to the project or venture.

Therefore, given the user's Meta Goal and their level of competence with respect to the relevant Micro Mindsets, the MindsetMap will suggest a particular tool, to be applied by the user and their coach, to:

- increase motivation
- increase competency
- help prioritize that Micro Mindset
- or strengthen the connection between that Micro Mindset and the corresponding area of Meta Mindset.

As with Meta and Macro Mindsets, the Success MindsetMap Premium Report provides the user with a map of their Micro Mindset zones of competence.

Micro Mindset Zones

			I enjoy it	I'm good at it	I'm spending time doing it
	SelfMotivator	interest	○		
	TeamMaker	genius	○	○	○
	ProductCreator	untapped excellence	○	○	
	MarketMaker	incompetence			○
	CompetenceBuilder	genius	○	○	○
	FinanSourcerer:	untapped excellence	○	○	
	VentureBuilder	competence		○	○
	MatchMaker	competence		○	○
	ReSourcerer	hobby	○		○

When combined with the ratings for the user's Meta Mindset and Macro Mindset, the Micro Mindset *zones of competence* provide a powerful insight into the types of tools and practices that can help to create a successful and sustainable project or venture. See Chapter 11 for an illustration of this dynamic.

CHAPTER

A MICRO MINDSET CASE STUDY: STEVE JOBS

As we pointed out earlier, in January of 2022 Apple Inc. became the first company ever to reach a $3 trillion market valuation. By any measure, Apple is one of the greatest success stories of the last century, and it owes a great deal of that success to the leadership of the brilliant and enigmatic Steve Jobs.

Jobs, who was also founder of NeXT Computers and instrumental in turning Pixar into a computer animation giant, was in many ways the epitome of the Silicon Valley entrepreneur. He stands out as one of the most successful people in modern history. More than 300 US patents are registered under his name, from computers to smartphones to electronic accessories and gadgets. There is no question that Stephen Paul Jobs left a significant mark on the modern world.

Much has been written about Steve Jobs, both before and since his death, and it is obvious that his success and the success of Apple were not based on him having a charming and likable personality. Jobs was frequently perceived as aggressive and demanding. *Fortune* magazine once wrote that he was "considered one of Silicon Valley's leading egomaniacs." A former colleague of Jobs once said that he "would have made an excellent king of France."

Certainly, Jobs' personal history did not make him an obvious candidate for such success. Born to an unwed mother and given up for adoption shortly after his birth, Jobs started his professional life as a first-year college dropout. How did he manage to make such impressive achievements? What were the key factors of his success?

From the perspective of the Success MindsetMap, Steve Jobs is a perfect example of finding a Role in which a powerful Ambition is put in the service of Mission and Vision. At his best, Steve Jobs was an example of a *transformational leader*. He was passionate and enthusiastic about what he did, created visions, and injected energy and motivation into the people he worked with. Driven, uncompromising, and motivational, Jobs inspired his coworkers and organizations to ever greater heights of creativity, driven by his own remarkable vision of how things might be.

Like Oprah Winfrey, who claimed that the most important discovery in all history was that "by changing your attitude, you can change your future," Jobs believed that mindset mattered most. In an interview from 1995 titled *The Secret to Life*, he explained:

When you grow up, you tend to get told that the world is the way it is and your life is just to live your life inside the world. Try not to bash into the walls too much. Try to have a nice family life. Have fun. Save a little money. But that's a very limited life. Life can be much broader once you discover one simple fact. And that is, everything around that you call life was made up by people who were no smarter than you. And you can change it. You can influence it. You can build your own things that other people can use.

And the minute that you understand that you can poke life, and that if you push in, something will pop out the other side; that you can change it, you can mold it.

That's maybe the most important thing. Is to shake off this erroneous notion that life is there and you're just going to live in it versus embrace it; change it; improve it; make your mark upon it.

And however you learn that, once you learn it, you'll want to change it and want to make it better, because life is messed up in a lot of ways. Once you learn that, you'll never be the same again.

STEVE JOBS' META MINDSET

Steve Jobs clearly operated from a mindset that he could change the world, improve it, and make his mark on it. These are aspects of Meta Mindset in the *Success MindsetMap Inventory*. *Meta Mindset* relates to success factors at the levels of *purpose* and *identity* and is about our fundamental attitude toward our work, our world, and our place in that world. The attributes comprising Meta Mindset include Passion, Vision, Mission, Ambition, and Role. A large part of Steve Jobs' and Apple's success has come from clarity about these guiding factors.

 **Passionate**

Central to Steve Jobs' Meta Mindset was Passion. Passion can be defined as *an intense desire or enthusiasm for something*. It is a relentless inner drive to find what it is that you care deeply about and for which you have talent and pursue it with all your heart. One of the things that the people who knew Steve Jobs all agree on is that he was passionate. As he claimed:

> *You've got to find what you love...The only way to be truly satisfied is to do what you believe is great work. And the only way to do great work is to love what you do.*

In fact, he went so far as to say:

> *Apple at its core, its core value is that we believe that people with passion can change the world for the better.*

For Jobs, passion was not only about doing great work and attaining satisfaction, but it was also the foundation for determination and perseverance. He explained:

> *People say you have to have a lot of passion for what you are doing and it's totally true. And the reason is because it is so hard that, if you don't, any rational person would give up. It's really hard and you have to do it over a sustained period of time. So, if you don't love it and you are not having fun doing it and if you don't really love it, you are going to give up.*

Finding what you love and living from the passion it generates is one of the major success factors that we have discovered in all successful entrepreneurs. The next step is to direct that passion outward toward a vision for the future.

Visionary

Another characteristic that everyone who knew Steve Jobs agrees upon is that he was visionary. As we have established, a *vision* is "a mental image of what the future will or could be like." It involves the ability to see beyond the confines of the "here and now" and imagine future possibilities and scenarios.

In the MindsetMap Inventory, we divide Vision into two forms of expression: destination and direction.

Destination

 When a person has a clear vision of the destination, they know exactly what they want to create in the longer-term future. As Jobs himself described it:

> *When I walk into a room and I want to talk about a product that hasn't been invented yet. I can see the product as if it's sitting there right in the center of the table. It's like what I've got to do is materialize it and bring it to life.*

In this regard, it is fascinating to note that Jobs' beloved iPad was the manifestation of a vision that he had from the earliest days of Apple. In 1983, Jobs gave a speech in which he said:

> *What we want to do is we want to put an incredibly great computer in a book that you can carry around with you and learn how to use in 20 minutes . . . And we really want to do it with a radio link in it so you don't have to hook up to anything and you're in communication with all of these larger databases and other computers.*

It would take almost thirty years for the technology to catch up with Jobs' vision.

Direction

 When you look far away, you cannot always see the result so clearly. Sometimes, the exact destination is not obvious, or, as with the iPad, there is a fair amount of uncertainty regarding the details of how the vision will finally manifest. In these cases, it is important to be clear about the direction, regardless of whether you know the ultimate destination.

Steve Jobs understood this well and took steps to actively instill that mindset in his team. As he put it:

> *There needs to be someone who is the keeper and reiterater of the vision; because there is just a ton of work to do and a lot of times when you have to walk a thousand miles and you take the first step, it looks like a long way. And it really helps if there is someone there who is saying, "Well, we are one step closer. The goal definitely exists. It's not just a mirage out there." So in a thousand and one little, and sometimes larger, ways, the vision needs to be reiterated. I do that a lot.*

 ## Purposeful

Being purposeful has to do with clarity about your mission – knowing what you stand for and why you are doing what you are doing, and the unique service you want to make through your venture. The mission of an individual within an organization is about their contribution to that organization and its vision. Similarly, an organization's mission will be defined with respect to the larger system of its customers and their needs.

There is a strong connection between Mission and Vision. Sometimes, the Vision guides and determines our Mission. At other times the mission is the source of new Visions. A well-formulated mission statement is generative. It defines what you are attempting to do, for whom, and for what purpose.

The basic structure of a good mission statement is:

To _____ (do what) for _____ (which larger system/customer)

in order to _____ (achieve what purpose).

Under Steve Jobs, Apple's mission statement was a classic example of this structure.

> To make a contribution to the world by making tools for the mind that advance humankind.

This statement is generative. It made it clear that Apple's activity was not just about personal computers; it was also about creating "tools for the mind that advance humankind." The development of the iPod is a good example of the generative nature of such an effective mission statement.

Jobs grew up in a period when rock and roll music was changing the world. He claimed that music was "good for the soul" and that he listened to music to stimulate his creative process of dreaming. He also saw the common love of music as a way of connecting to a whole new generation of technology users.

Because of his passion for the power of music, Steve Jobs took a very active role in the iPod project scheduling frequent meetings with the designers. During these meetings, he would tell them in detail what issues he had with the device, whether it was the interface, sound quality, or the size of the scroll wheel.

For Jobs, the iPod epitomized the vision and mission of Apple. He saw it as something that "really changed the world" by helping to "bring music back into people's lives in a really meaningful way." As he put it:

> If there was ever a product that catalyzed what's Apple's reason for being, it's (the iPod). Because it combines Apple's incredible technology base with Apple's legendary ease of use with Apple's awesome design... it's like, this is what we do. So, if anybody was ever wondering why is Apple on the Earth, I would hold this up as a good example.

Jobs' references to "Apple's incredible technology base," "Apple's legendary ease of use," and "Apple's awesome design" are clear and concise answers to the questions, "What is your unique contribution and service with respect to the vision for your customers? What are the special resources, capabilities, and actions that you will develop and apply to reach your vision for your customers?" One of the great strengths of Apple as an organization has been the clear sense of Mission instilled by Steve Jobs as a leader.

 Ambitious

Ambition is an important complement to vision and mission. It is a mindset that is focused on achieving concrete results which meet clear criteria within a specified time frame. Ambition is defined as "a strong desire to do or to achieve something, typically requiring determination and hard work." Ambitions typically arise from the drive for growth and mastery.

Steve Jobs was clearly highly ambitious. In fact, he is the person that we chose to represent the mindset of Ambition for the MindsetMap Inventory. An iconic example of the Meta Mindset quality of ambition is Jobs' statement that he wanted to "put a dent in the universe."

Jobs strove to promote this mindset in his coworkers as well. He was notoriously demanding and exacting down to every detail. In his words:

> We have an environment where excellence is really expected . . .
> My best contribution is not settling for anything but really good stuff,
> in all the details. That's my job – to make sure everything is great.
>
> My job is to not be easy on people. My job is to make them better.
>
> My job is to pull things together from different parts of the company and
> clear the ways and get the resources for the key projects. And to take
> these great people we have and to push them and make them even
> better, coming up with more aggressive visions of how it could be.

Ambition is the engine that drives the mission towards the vision. Jobs had a deep understanding of this and even introduced the notion of "evangelism" into the company to describe the type of fervor he expected people to have for the products they were developing at Apple.

People who worked closely with Steve Jobs generally acknowledge that it could be "very challenging," at least at times. However, if you asked, "Would you do it again?" a majority would say, "Absolutely." This was frequently because they felt like they grew or improved as a result of working with him. In the words of one Apple employee:

> I was incredibly grateful for the apparently harsh treatment Steve had dished out the first time. He forced me to work harder, and in the end I did a much better job than I would have otherwise. I believe it is one of the most important aspects of Steve Jobs' impact on Apple: he had little or no patience for anything but excellence from himself or others.

 ## Accountable

Accountability and Role relate to the position an individual, team, or organization has with respect to others in their market or environment. If passion is the fuel and ambition is the engine, then role is the vehicle in which you travel the road of your mission in the direction of the Vision.

The questions related to Role have a lot to do with *who* you are within your ecosystem. Who do you serve? Who do you work with? Who do you work for? etc. Your answers to these questions forge the relationships you have and develop with respect to customers, coworkers, partners, stakeholders, and competitors.

The mindset that guides you to choosing or creating the most effective role is one that is constantly assessing key competencies and characteristics you need to be able to best progress on your mission and achieve your ambitions. It also involves thinking, acting, and deciding in ways that are aligned with who you are within your environment.

Steve Jobs had a very clear sense of his role and the role that Apple had within its environment. Robert's father-in-law, who was a senior technology manager for IBM in the 1980s, refers to Steve Jobs as an *orchestrator of evolution*. He saw Jobs' major strength as having been "a selector, evolver and integrator of good ideas" rather than a developer of fundamental technologies. Jobs' embracing of this role of "orchestrator of evolution" in support of the Vision, Mission, and Ambition of his ventures was clearly a major key to his success.

Having a comprehensive understanding of your role allows you to effectively work together with others in your ecosystem to further your Mission and fulfill the Vision. As he described it:

> *I felt it the first time when I visited a school. They had third and fourth graders in a classroom full of Apple IIs. I spent a few hours there and I saw these third and fourth graders growing up completely differently than I did because they had this machine.*
>
> *And what hit me about it was, here was this machine that a very few people designed; about four in the case of the Apple II. And then they gave it to some people that didn't know how to design it, but they knew how to make it, to manufacture it. They could make a whole bunch of them. And then they gave it to some people who didn't know how to design it or manufacture it, but they knew how to distribute it. They gave it to people that didn't know how to design, distribute or manufacture it, but they knew how to write software for it.*
>
> *Gradually this sort of inverse pyramid grew, and when it finally got into the hands of a lot of people, it blossomed out of this tiny little seed. It seemed like an incredible amount of leverage. And it all started with just an idea. And here was this idea taken through all of these stages, resulting in a classroom full of kids growing up with some insights and some fundamentally different experiences which I thought might be very beneficial to their lives because of this germ of an idea a few years before.*
>
> *And that is an incredible feeling; to know that you had something to do with it and to know that it can be done. To know that you can plant something in the world and it will grow and change the world ever so slightly.*

STEVE JOBS' MACRO MINDSET

While Meta Mindset gives you big picture clarity, Macro Mindset supports the ongoing habits and routines necessary to realize your goals and achieve sustainable success. Macro Mindset relates to the mental disciplines and practices required to bring focus to the big picture of your venture and the steps necessary to put into action to achieve it. Steve Jobs was well aware of the importance of this. As he pointed out:

> To turn really interesting ideas and fledgling technologies into a company that can continue to innovate for years, it requires a lot of disciplines.

These disciplines involve developing such capabilities as managing your energy and focus, seeking honest and frequent feedback, scanning for opportunities, dealing effectively with risks and adversity, and recharging and balancing yourself. Jobs was aware of all this and put routines in place to bring attention to these various issues as the following example illustrates:

> What we do every Monday is we review the whole business. We look at what we sold the week before. We look at every single product under development, products we're having trouble with, products where the demand is larger than we can make. All the stuff in development, we review. And we do it every single week.

The following are other examples of how Jobs approached the various areas of Macro Mindset:

Energizer – *Maintaining Energy and Focus*

Do what you are passionate about and invest a lot of energy and focus into making what you want happen.

> *We don't get a chance to do that many things, and every one should be really excellent. Because this is our life. And we've all chosen to do this with our lives. So it better be damn good. It better be worth it.*

> *You've got to find what you love...The only way to be truly satisfied is to do what you believe is great work. And the only way to do great work is to love what you do.*

> *People think focus means saying yes to the thing you've got to focus on. But that's not what it means at all. It means saying no to the hundred other good ideas that there are. You have to pick carefully. I'm actually as proud of many of the things we haven't done as the things we have done.*

 Seeker – *Getting Frequent and Honest Feedback*

Seek feedback and have established ways to get honest and frequent feedback.

> *So when a good idea comes, you know, part of my job is to move it around, just see what different people think, get people talking about it, argue with people about it, get ideas moving among that group of 100 people, get different people together to explore different aspects of it quietly, and, you know – just explore things.*

> *We figure out what we want. And I think we're pretty good at having the right discipline to think through whether a lot of other people are going to want it, too.*

Scanner – *Continually Scanning for Opportunities*

Constantly scan for opportunities and invest time to create them.

> *There's an old Wayne Gretzky quote that I love: "I skate to where the puck is going to be, not where it has been." And we've always tried to do that at Apple. Since the very, very beginning. And we always will.*

Persister – *Staying Determined and Resilient*

Be aware of risks and potential problems and don't get discouraged or distracted in the face of adversity and negative feedback.

> *Your time is limited, so don't waste it living someone else's life. Don't be trapped by dogma – which is living with the results of other people's thinking. Don't let the noise of other's opinions drown out your own inner voice. And most important, have the courage to follow your heart and intuition. They somehow already know what you truly want to become. Everything else is secondary.*

> *Sometimes when you're in the middle of one of these crises, you're not sure you're going to make it to the other end. But we've always made it, and so we have a certain degree of confidence, although sometimes you wonder. I think the key thing is that we're not all terrified at the same time.*

Recharger – *Remaining Grounded and Resourceful*

Be internally grounded and resourceful and have your ways of recharging and balancing yourself and practice them daily.

> *For the past thirty-eight years, I have looked in the mirror every morning and asked myself: "If today were the last day of my life, would I want to do what I am about to do today?" And whenever the answer has been "No" for too many days in a row, I know I need to change something.*

STEVE JOBS' MICRO MINDSET

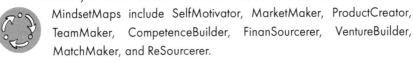

As we have established, *Micro Mindset* produces and guides the specific actions necessary to build a sustainable venture. The main Micro Mindsets in Success MindsetMaps include SelfMotivator, MarketMaker, ProductCreator, TeamMaker, CompetenceBuilder, FinanSourcerer, VentureBuilder, MatchMaker, and ReSourcerer.

According to the MindsetMap, what takes someone from a level of excellence to genius is not only that they enjoy, are good at, and spend time doing a particular competence, but that it is also connected to their passion, vision, and ambition.

Clearly, creating something remarkable or exceptional will require at least a level of excellence, if not genius, in several of these areas of Micro Mindset, and most likely a minimum level of competence in all of them. Steve Jobs certainly was an acknowledged genius as a ProductCreator. The unprecedented success of Apple under his leadership, however, was also due to a level of at least excellence in the areas of TeamMaker, Competence Builder, MatchMaker, and Resourcerer.

 ProductCreator – *Seeing the Future Before It Becomes Obvious*

The mindset of the ProductCreator is to anticipate and fulfill customer needs and desires by imagineering innovative and empowering solutions (products and services). This was one of Jobs' strongest areas of competence. A major part of Jobs' success was his ability to position his businesses and their products at the forefront of the technology industry by foreseeing and setting trends with respect to their market and connecting them to his vision.

For example, when asked how much money he spent on market research to develop the iPad, Jobs famously replied, "None. It's not the consumers' job to know what they want." He didn't need to do market research, he claimed, because he already knew it would succeed. Jobs' ability to have his "finger on the pulse" of his marketplace and link those signals to his vision was one of his most critical success factors.

As an illustration, Jobs revealed that he began developing the iPad in 2004, but realized that it wasn't the right time to launch it as processor speed, screen resolutions, and wireless networks of that time were not good enough to make it successful. Instead of hurrying up the launch, Jobs waited until all the ingredients of the product were ready to give the level of performance necessary to be successful. He temporarily put the effort on hold, realizing that the ideas would work just as well in a mobile smartphone. He viewed the iPhone as a miniature version of the iPad that could be enlarged when the pieces were all in place.

By 2009, he had made almost all the preparations for launching the tablet; everything was in place from screens, processors and the all-important mobile networks. After the success of iPhone, Jobs was convinced that people would love the tablet he had been designing. And the rest is history.

 ## TeamMaker – A Passion for Excellence

The mindset of the TeamMaker is to attract and give focus to people by fostering synergy, complementarity, and alignment. The TeamMaker mindset is geared toward assembling and providing direction and support to team members and encouraging team cooperation. As Walt Disney pointed out, "You can dream, create, design, and build the most wonderful place in the world, but it takes people to make the dream a reality."

While it is no secret that Steve Jobs could be notoriously difficult to work with, he was also equally inspiring. According to his biographer Walter Isaacson:

> *Everyone was eager to talk about Steve. They all had stories to tell, and they loved to tell them. Even those who told me about his rough manner put it in the context of how inspiring he could be . . . He could be petulant and rough, but this was driven by his passion and pursuit of perfection. He liked people to stand up to him, and he said that brutal honesty was required to be part of his team. And the teams he built became extremely loyal and inspired.*

One of the most common statements I have heard from people who worked closely with Jobs is that "It is difficult to find someone who actually liked Steve Jobs, but everyone respected him." There is no doubt of his clear commitment to the values he espoused.

Robert's former father-in-law, who was a carpet salesman in the Silicon Valley during the early days of Apple, tells a revealing story about going to Apple to sell carpet. To his surprise, Steve Jobs came into the presentation. According to Robert's father-in law, Jobs asked ten times more questions any other customer he had before or since that time. Jobs wanted to know the details of how the carpets were manufactured, what they were made of, and why they were better than other options. Jobs inquired about the company, its suppliers, and why he should choose them instead of someone else. While Robert's father-in-law was impressed, he eventually found himself starting to wonder, "Don't you have a company to run?"

It is quite likely that Jobs did not really intend to micromanage to the level of choosing the carpets for the company. Rather, he was probably role modeling a Micro Mindset to the other Apple employees that were at the meeting. As Jobs explained it:

> If [people] are working in an environment where excellence is expected, then they will do excellent work without anything but self-motivation. I'm talking about an environment in which excellence is noticed and respected and is in the culture. If you have that, you don't have to tell people to do excellent work. They understand it from their surroundings.

In his best-selling biography of Steve Jobs, Walter Isaacson includes a quote from Jobs that provides insight into how Jobs created alignment and team cooperation around his mindset. In the quote, Jobs explains how his family decided to choose a particular washing machine for their home. Though one would think it is a seemingly trivial purchase, Jobs' explanation of how the decision was made illustrates how he passed on his passion for excellence to those around him.

> It turns out that the Americans make washers and dryers all wrong. The Europeans make them much better – but they take twice as long to do clothes! It turns out they wash them with about a quarter as much water and clothes end up with a less detergent on them. Most important, they don't trash your clothes. They use a lot less soap, a lot less water, but they come out much cleaner, much softer and they last a lot longer.

We spent some time in our family talking about what's the trade-off we want to make. We ended up talking a lot about design, but also a lot about the values of our family. Did we care more about getting our wash done in an hour versus an hour and a half? Or did we care most about clothes feeling really soft and lasting longer?
Did we care about using a quarter of the water? We spent about two weeks talking about this every night at the dinner table.

Jobs' focus on *design* and the *values* of the family were key themes in his pattern of success. But this attention to detail and emphasis on excellence is only part of the story. He also encouraged creativity, fostered collective intelligence, and actively facilitated a culture of competence.

 CompetenceBuilder – *Orchestrating Evolution*

The mindset of the CompetenceBuilder is to coach, be an example, and provide opportunities for team members to grow in order to increase competency. The focus of the CompetenceBuilder mindset is on encouraging and providing opportunities for team members to learn and grow.

Jobs experimented with changes in organizational structure at Apple and when he started NeXT he abandoned conventional corporate structures altogether. Instead, the company was organized as a "community" with "members" rather than employees. There were only two different salaries at NeXT until the early 1990s, and which one people received depended upon when they joined the company as opposed to their position in the organization.

The success of Pixar is also considered to be a direct result of Jobs' attitudes and behaviors, including his inspiring of employees and his confidence in them. Jobs established an environment without strict management practices or a rigid hierarchy. He built a social workplace that encouraged cooperation, teamwork, and open conversation between all levels of employees. The quality and aspirations of employees he hired ensured a high level of creativity and imagination of all individuals working at the company. Pixar personnel are known for having a deeper commitment to their work and creations than their desire for money.

Steve Jobs' unwavering commitment to the achievement of the larger vision and his constant focus on innovation and excellence were key success factors in his repeated success as a leader and in the success of his ventures. According to John Lasseter, chief creative officer at Pixar and Walt Disney Animation Studios, and Edwin Catmull, current president of Walt Disney Animation Studios and Pixar Animation Studios:

> *Steve was an extraordinary visionary, our very dear friend, and our guiding light of the Pixar family. He saw the potential of what Pixar could be before the rest of us, and beyond what anyone ever imagined. Steve took a chance on us and believed in our crazy dream of making computer animated films; the one thing he always said was to "make it great." He is why Pixar turned out the way we did and his strength, integrity, and love of life has made us all better people. He will forever be part of Pixar's DNA.*

 ## MatchMaker – *The Power of Win-Win*

The mindset of the MatchMaker is to seek other ventures that resonate with the values and bigger vision of their own venture and that complement one another's business strengths (through sharing, combining, or exchanging) to build win-win relationships. This is another Micro Mindset that Jobs was able to embrace, and one that likely saved Apple.

Twelve years after the introduction of the Macintosh, in 1996, when Jobs re-emerged as CEO of Apple (after NeXT Computer was bought by Apple), the company was struggling and near bankruptcy. In 1985, Jobs had been removed from managerial duties at Apple as result of a power struggle with John Sculley, who Jobs himself had recruited as Apple's CEO. As a consequence, Jobs resigned from the company that he had created. Eleven years later, Jobs returned to a company that was on the verge of failure. One of Jobs' first actions was to arrange a strategic partnership with the software giant Microsoft with whom Apple, under Sculley, had been engaged in a drawn-out and costly legal battle over patent rights. In 1997, at the Boston Macworld Expo, Jobs took the stage to deliver one of his famous keynote speeches. He stunned his audience, for whom the world had become defined by the struggle between the "underdog" Apple and the increasingly "all-powerful"

Microsoft Corporation, with the following announcement:

> *Apple lives in an ecosystem and it needs help from other partners;*
> *it needs to help other partners. And relationships that are destructive*
> *don't help anybody in this industry as it is today. So during the last*
> *several weeks we have looked at some of the relationships, and one*
> *has stood out as a relationship that hasn't been going so well, but*
> *that has the potential, I think, to be great for both companies.*
> *And I'd like to announce one of our first partnerships today, a very*
> *very meaningful one. And that is one with Microsoft. . .*
>
> *We have to let go of this notion that for Apple to win, Microsoft has*
> *to lose . . . the era of setting this up as a competition between Apple*
> *and Microsoft is over as far as I'm concerned. This is about getting*
> *Apple healthy and . . . about Apple being able to make incredibly*
> *great contributions to the computer industry, to be healthy*
> *and prosper again.*

The deal set up several arrangements for the cross-licensing of patents. It guaranteed that Microsoft would continue to release Microsoft Office products for the Mac platform. Apple began to make Microsoft's Internet Explorer the default browser on all new Mac products. Microsoft also bought $150m of non-voting Apple shares at market prices with the agreement not to sell them for three years. This meant Microsoft was now also a stakeholder in addition to being a partner and had a vested interest in seeing Apple's share price increase, rather than collapse. When news of the deal reached the market, Apple's stock rose by 35% overnight!

This example shows the power of partnerships and why they are such a key part of the Circle of Success. And, again, it was Jobs' clarity about his role as an *orchestrator of evolution* and his commitment to the bigger vision and mission of Apple that was at the basis of the move. His claim that "This is about getting Apple healthy and . . . about Apple being able to make incredibly great contributions to the computer industry, to be healthy and prosper again," is a clear statement of the link between putting ambition into the service of the greater identity and mission of the company.

ReSourcerer –*Expanding the Mission*

The mindset of the Resourcerer is about recognizing, exploring. and implementing significant synergies with the products, services, competencies, etc., of other complementary ventures in order to expand and leverage resources.

Jobs' competence with respect to this mindset is particularly well illustrated by the development of the iPod, a product that changed both Apple and the entire music business. Before its introduction, MP3 players were the realm of small companies with limited funds who were unable to provide content. After the iPod, the entire industry evolved and grew to the point where the largest computer companies in the world have major interests in the digital music industry.

When the iPod was designed, Apple lacked the internal resources necessary to make an attractive music device. Instead of trying to develop a whole new set of capabilities, Apple licensed the software platform from a 3rd party, PortalPlayer. Similarly, it acquired software from the outside to build iTunes and hired music software experts and hardware engineers from outside the company, integrating them with a team of Apple veterans. Apple contracted another company, Pixo, to help design and implement the user interface under the direct supervision of Steve Jobs.

Conclusion

Steve Jobs' role of "orchestrator of evolution," supported by his genius as a ProductCreator and his excellence as TeamMaker, CompetenceBuilder, MatchMaker and ReSourcerer, allowed him to reach his ambition to "put a dent in the universe," stay ahead of the curve and keep moving to where "the puck is going to be." This was all in the service of the vision of empowered individuals using "insanely great" technology and products, and in support of the mission *"to make a contribution to the world by making tools for the mind that advance humankind."*

CHAPTER

THE SIX STEPS OF MINDSETMAPS™ COACHING AND SOME METHODOLOGY CONSIDERATIONS

Before we introduce you to the MindsetMaps COACH+ process of, we would like to speak to a point that comes up regularly when we talk to our clients or to experienced coaches. This question about MindsetMaps is related to the so-called subjectivity of personal rating and perception. A related idea is that to make the Success MindsetMap Inventory more objective, we could create a kind of 360 type assessment in addition to the self-evaluation. However, there is a significant reason why we have created the inventory as it is today based on self-evaluation and not in a peer or 360-degree approach. We are convinced that we get more reliable data this way and we are not alone with this view in the world of research. We would like to quote Marcus Buckingham, known as the world's most prominent researcher on strengths and leadership at work, and who today leads research at the ADP Research Institute:

> *The data generated from a 360 survey is bad. It's always bad. And since the data is bad, no matter how well-intended your coaching, how insightful your feedback, how coherent your leadership model, you are likely leading your leaders astray.*

Now, what does he mean by "bad" you might wonder? His point is that when you want a reliable opinion about a topic, researchers put together a random, representative sample of people in terms of race, qualifications, demographics etc., so they avoid getting "bad" skewed data. When you do 360 surveys, that's exactly what should happen as well, but it doesn't, since we go to the very specific people who work for or with the person we appraise, which will make the data skewed. Most of these people will either withhold their true viewpoint even in anonymity (since it is always easy to guess who said what due to specifics in the comments) or they have very strong personal views which are based on isolated incidents or hearsay and gossip that is going around about a specific person.

Another issue with evaluating others is that for someone to rate someone reliably on, let's say, listening skills or clarity of Vision or Ambition, they themselves should be reliable experts on that particular subject, skill, or competence. For example, they should be very clear on the Vision and Ambition of the organization or person to be able to evaluate someone else's clarity on it. Otherwise, the ratings will be subjective and more about the person who rates than the person being rated. As they evaluate someone when they believe they themselves are clearer on what the vision is, they will rate the other person low or, vice versa, they will rate the other person high on vision if they think the other person is clearer than they are. And when you add up a bunch of very subjective data, you get a big pile of "bad data." It will be a version of "elevated gossip."

People are not very reliable raters of others; however, they are better raters of themselves as they know more about what goes on inside their mind more than anyone else, especially when they get some help from a coach who challenges their ratings, asks for evidence, and helps them to calibrate and use the scale the right way. As Carl Rogers said, "I have come to feel that the only learning which significantly influences behavior is self-discovered, self-appropriated learning." Therefore, we found that it is best if those who take the MindsetMap Inventory take it as self-rating and then engage in self-discovery discussions with a mindset coach. At the end, they may adjust their ratings, but the insights they achieve through such a process will be far more powerful then any feedback they would be given by others.

As you will see when we introduce the six steps, this also has to do with our process where we often suggest that the coach and coachee take the inventory together in a longer session, so the coach can help the coachee to calibrate the accuracy of their ratings and yet let the coachee self-discover by answering each of the questions.

The Six Steps of the COACH+ MindsetMaps Coaching Process

So, why have a process for MindsetMap coaching? Isn't every client and team different? Is it possible to define a sequence of steps that should be followed in a linear fashion? Yes, every client and team is different. It is also true that coaching is rarely a linear development. However, we believe that the question, "What does good looks like?" is vital and relevant to defining an approach or methodology. Based on our close to eighty years of combined coaching experience, we have outlined what we think "good looks like" called the COACH+ process. This process consists of six steps. These steps are not meant to be understood as a strict script, but they are a good progression towards what we believe is a good standard for applying the MindsetMaps methodology. These six steps are:

1. COACH state – creating the necessary psychological safety and rapport as well as a generative state as foundation for the coaching to take place.

 2. Objectives and opportunities – deciding "where to tap" and what is the difference that will make the most difference for the coachee in terms of reaching their goal.

 3. Action planning – deciding what actions, milestones, and timeline are necessary for the client to achieve their goal.

 4. Concrete action steps – deciding what smaller bite steps will make sense and where to start in simple, concrete action terms.

 5. Handling obstacles – obstacles will inevitably appear at some point, and this step is about anticipating or encountering and transforming whatever stands in the way of the coachee achieving their objective.

 6. Provide accountability and support –supporting the coachee at the time "when the rubber hits the road." It is necessary for accountability and tracking progress for both the coachee and coach.

You will find that sometimes, certain steps can happen in a different order. For example, obstacles may come up earlier than in step 5. You will also find that this is circular process that you may go through several times with a client.

6 Steps of Mindset Coaching

We like to say that state matters more than script! Another important notion is that what happens before and after the actual coaching session is just as crucial as the content of a session.

STEP 1 – COACH STATE

This step is about establishing a high-quality inner state for both the coach and coachee, so they can both be at their best during the work.

For us, a high quality inner state has the following characteristics:

Centered vs **C**onstricted and closed
Open vs **R**eactive
Aware and attentive vs **A**nalysis paralysis
Connected vs **S**eparate
Holding and hospitable vs **H**ostile, hurt, or hateful

It is often a good way of building rapport to ask a client if they already have a practice of putting themselves in a good state and then go through that method together by letting the coachee lead. Having said that, in a first session, the coach has to often introduce the practice and go first. Eventually, a COACH state exercise can become the way to start every session and be a way to regain one's best self if something difficult occurs during the session.

This first step is hard to pin down in terms of an exact sequence of sub steps, but there are some key ingredients to keep in mind. First, it all starts with the coach who needs to establish and self-calibrate their own COACH state prior to starting a session. As is pointed out during security demonstrations on airplanes, one needs to put on one's own oxygen mask first to be able to take care of someone else. Once our own COACH state is established, we can take time to establish a COACH state for a coachee. This will be essential to establish a safe COACH container at the outset. Such a COACH container can be established by shifting states and building a deep rapport that cements the right foundation and facilitates an open dialogue with transformational potential.

STEP 2 – OBJECTIVES AND OPPORTUNITIES

The exact form of this step will depend on whether a coachee has taken the inventory together with their coach. If they have, they have already gone through a similar process to what is described below. If a coachee took the inventory without a coach, there will be a conversational review of the results as per the Premium Report.

At this point the coach is looking to establish where to tap, i.e., what area they should focus on to make the biggest difference for their client. The power of the inventory is that it takes the coach and client down a path that leads to finding the "It factor" for the coaching and development focus.

The goal for the coach in this step is to determine key patterns, both cognitive and somatic, as potential areas of focus for coaching. The question the coach is trying to answer is, "Which area should have priority to make the biggest possible progress?" As the coach is looking for a deeper understanding of their client's current mindset, we strongly recommend the use of multiple intelligences, including verbal, somatic, and imagery, rather than just using more left brain, conscious mind chatter. This is where the MindsetMaps work connects to the so-called generative change approach defined by Steve Gilligan and Robert.

Ultimately, the coach needs to prioritize. A key point here is Micro and Meta Mindset interrelations. If there is a key gap in Meta Mindset, the coach should prioritize helping with that before aiming to focus on micro actions. This is something we teach in detail in our MindsetMaps coach certification.

STEP 3 – ACTION PLANNING

Although this step could also take many forms, there are some basic prerequisites for it to be successful. At this point, the coach needs to have established a clear shared understanding with their coachee on what the current and desired states are. We have found that it is vital at this stage to help the coachee develop a real felt sense of their future state in their body.

Action planning is often connected with the Macro Mindset habits of success, as many of the actions will require continued commitment and sustained energy from the coachee. Staying connected to passion, getting high quality feedback, and staying resilient and courageous play very prominent roles in achieving a desired outcome.

STEP 4 – CONCRETE ACTION STEPS

This the step where the rubber meets the road, as the saying goes. At this point, the coach has established a critical path with their coachee to achieve their desired outcomes. Therefore, this step will include a review of Micro Mindset requirements for implementing the concrete action steps on the path. A key aspect of that work is, again, to go beyond verbal leftbrain intelligence and use multiple intelligences, including somatic movement and imagery. The review will include permutations and zones of competence, check from waste of time all the way to zone of genius, and draw conclusions in terms of development, delegation, and bringing in support. At the end of this step there should be a decision on relevant actions with the coachee. Those actions are best defined in the form of a positive statement, and should be simple, specific, and achievable within the coachee's range of control, and last but not least, ecological.

STEP 5 – HANDLING OBSTACLES

The only thing we know for sure about obstacles is that there will be obstacles. As experienced coaches, we always get quite concerned if a coachee cannot identify or anticipate any obstacles as this is typically a sign of overconfidence, naivety, or a blind spot. Obstacles may appear at any time during our coaching process, from the beginning to the end. With some coachees, you will encounter them immediately when trying to establish a high-quality COACH state. With others, they will come when you are doing the action planning. One place that they are very likely to appear is when the coachee starts taking first actions steps agreed with you.

Obstacles have many forms and are always an interesting mix of internal and external circumstances. We believe there is an inner and outer game element of any obstacle or barrier. For example, a person may need to talk to an important stakeholder who is very busy and has little time on their schedule, which is an objective external difficulty. At the same time, our coachee may procrastinate scheduling the meeting due to fear of rejection, which is the inner game part. Successful coaching will help the coachee tackle both the inner and outer elements.

The challenge is often to pinpoint the most relevant inner game element of an issue at hand, which is not easy. It will need to come from the coachee, but the coach's intuition, experience, and questions will play a big role. The most important success factor here is for the coachee to be in a generative COACH state, to be able tune into their deeper understanding of the inner game part of an obstacle and the best resources. The Micro Mindset inventory results are very helpful to identify the key gaps to address and what obstacles may be connected with those critical areas, and MindsetMaps will direct the coach to these specific areas. Calibration will also play an important role here, as the coach needs to ask for evidence of the Micro Mindset ratings to double check that a coachee's understanding is accurate.

STEP 6 – + PROVIDE ACCOUNTABILITY

Once the coachee starts taking the specific actions steps agreed to achieve their goals, the focus coaching moves to accountability, which is one of the most important reasons as to why people reach out to a coach in the first place. They want someone to hold their hands or hold them accountable. The trick with this is that people also tend to defer responsibility to the coach by doing that and claim "that you were supposed to hold me accountable for not doing what we agreed." Accountability is a fundamental part of the coach's work, but it needs to be carefully and masterfully delivered so that it is the coachee who ultimately maintains responsibility and commitment to their outcome, while there is also a clear way to track progress.

This step is about how the coach and coachee will know that the desired change was achieved. Concrete signpost will have to be defined in terms of outcomes, indicators, behaviors and feelings. The Success MindetMaps Inbentory is a great way to note progress so we recommend taking the inventory several times during a coaching process to be able to do that. This is another fundamental difference compared to personality profiles which are to be taken once. The MindsetMap is meant to visualize current and desired states and then serve as a way of checking on the shift.

The next chapter provides an example of how the MindsetMap Inventory and COACH+ process can be applied with a client.

A CASE STUDY ABOUT THE APPLICATION OF THE SUCCESS MINDSETMAPS INVENTORY

OVERVIEW

We would like to present the case of how we applied the SFM Success MindsetMaps Inventory with the managing director of the subsidiary company of a large *Fortune 500* multinational organization. For this chapter, we are going to switch the style of the book to storytelling mode to give you a feel for actual conversations between a MindsetMaps coach and coachee and how the SMI works in practice.

INTRODUCING COACH FRED AND HIS CLIENT, JOHN

Meet Fred. Fred is a consultant and executive team coach living and working in New York City, arguably the most competitive city in the world. Right now, he is sitting in a very modern office in the Dumbo office complex in NYC. The windows overlook the water and he can see the Brooklyn Bridge and the Manhattan skyline on the other side. Not a bad building to have corner office in, he is thinking to himself, feeling somewhat jealous.

Meet John. John leads a division management team of eight people at the US subsidiary company of large global business headquartered in Sweden. The parent company provides a certain framework in terms of brand, values, and high-level strategy but is not deeply involved in the running of the US business. The people on the team come from two different companies and two different cultures. Three people on the team come from the Swedish company, while most are American, including the division head. Each team member also leads teams. Four of the team members also have very high-level key account management responsibilities.

After a brief check in, John launches into sharing his frustrations about his team to Fred. "Their conversion rates, i.e., turning prospects into contracted agreements, are very low, and the sales cycles are way too long," he states, visibly irritated.

Fred learns that John has been tasked with creating a high-performing team and culture in the subsidiary he leads. The goals John has received from his superiors are:

- Increase cohesiveness in the team and get rid of legacy thinking.

- Get rid of silo thinking and bring in more collaboration.

- Build clarity around what good looks like in terms of management and turn managers into effective leaders who coach.

- Ultimately increase sales by reducing sales cycles and increasing conversion rates.

John explains he decided to engage a team coach so he can tackle these goals, and he selected Fred because he believes Fred brings a multicultural background to the table that will be very important.

The following is an excerpt of their conversation in the kick-off meeting of the project:

John: I am still very unhappy with my team. I am not sure they are the right people. I can tell you what's wrong with each of them. Should I? (He doesn't wait for answers and continues.)

Tim, the head of sales, is the most talented, but he comes from very far away. He used to think people were machines and that emotions had no place in business. He used not to listen and be very forceful and direct. Today, he is one of my best leaders with a coaching style. He has come a long way, but he still has some blind spots around trust and vulnerability.

Anna, our CFO, is a superwoman. She wants everything and everyone to be perfect. She is extremely resilient but has a one-track mind approach with no tolerance for others. She only cares about her division and no one else matters to her.

Peter, our head of operations, is a great functional expert, but quite introverted and focused on his team. He has trouble communicating in a language that's not full of jargon and understandable to others.

Marie, our customer service leader, is very detail-oriented and constantly acts like a victim. She is quite introverted, reserved, and quiet in our meetings. We don't notice if she is not there, to be honest.

Fred: This is all useful information, John. Sorry to stop you thinking for a moment, but it might be helpful if I share a few key principles that I use in my work. One of the key axioms in Success MindsetMaps is that we work from the inside out in terms of how to create impact on key stakeholders. So far, the goals and the information about your team seem to be all about fixing the people on the team and correcting their behavior, etc.

As I truly believe change must come from the top and that symptoms come from a systemic interference which includes the leader, I would like to ask you a few questions, if that's alright with you.

John – Sure, go ahead.

Fred: I believe that mindset produces the actions we take which, in turn, bring about resulting outcomes and achievements. Let's explore your mindset and the goals a little more. What's your single most important focus (meta goal) for, say, the next two years?

J: My key goal is to scale the business and build robust processes for execution and effective coaching to fix our culture.

F: May I ask how satisfied you feel in this role currently on a scale of 1 to 10?

J: Well, I would say it is a 5 or 6, more like a 5.

F: Can you share more about that?

J: Sure, though I am not yet quite sure how this is relevant. In any case, I feel I can only utilize about 50% of my skills and competencies here. I don't think that I matter to the board other than being a cog in the machine that's supposed to deliver the bottom line. My team is full of functional experts, but we are not a team together. They don't learn from each other and are just focused on getting their jobs done. I am trying to act as a conductor for a team of people who don't see themselves as an orchestra.

F: I hear you. That must be challenging and frustrating. One thing that can unite a team is clarity on a vision of what the future should look like if you succeed together. As a starting point, what's your personal vision, say, five years from now?

J: I am not sure I will be working here five years from now. I don't know. I think my dream would be that we are a team of passionately driven top-class professionals who share the same purpose of wanting to bring alternative energy to every business in America, or something to that end.

143

F: I see. I think clarity on your vision, ambition, and purpose as well as goals will strongly influence how you should lead this team. What would you say if we were to use an instrument to map out your current mindset and, by choosing your focus, we could then contrast it with an ideal mindset that will support the achievement of your focus? I have a tool that was created based on decades of international research and modeling of successful conscious leaders. Would that be something that would interest you?

J: That sounds interesting. I was hoping we could start working on the team right away, but I can see that what you are suggesting makes sense. If I am unclear about my trajectory, it will be hard to rally the team around it.

F: Spot on. The SFM Success MindsetMap Inventory is a tool that was designed to help an individual or a team understand their mindset and then figure out how to adjust or align it to achieve their goals.

When the tool was created, the founders applied the distinctions of Success Factor Modeling, which is methodology seeking to analyze the connection between mindset, actions people take, and the outcomes that arise as result. It is an approach to help businesspeople understand what is the difference that makes the difference that leads to successful outcomes. As part of this work, several well-known entrepreneurs including Elon Musk of Tesla, Steve Jobs of Apple, Richard Branson of the Virgin Group, Jeff Bezos of Amazon.com, Howard Schultz of Starbucks, Muhammed Yunus of Grameen Bank, and Anita Roddick of The Body Shop, were analyzed. Many others were also interviewed and the inventory is a synthesis of all this work.

J: Wait, let me stop you there. Are you saying that these people are supposed to be my ideals for good leadership? Because I have some reservations about Bezos, and Schultz for that matter.

F: Not at all. Personality and mindset are not the same. The tool does not suggest anyone becomes like Steve Jobs or models his personality. It does suggest that his mindset, and in particular his ambition, allowed him to create an amazingly successful company. Hence, he is the archetype for the Meta Mindset quality of ambition in the inventory. This inventory helps you identify your particular aptitudes and tendencies and to know which ones you need to prioritize and strengthen to take yourself, your company, and your team to the next level.

After this conversation, John and Fred agreed they would take the mindset inventory together in their next session. Fred thought it would be better that way, rather than leaving John to take it on his own without guidance.

John and Fred meet to take the online MindsetMap Inventory

F: As we go through the online inventory, I will be your guide for the questions and I will help you calibrate your answers and ratings. Does that sound good?

J: Yes. I read the overview of the three levels of Mindset – Meta, Macro and Micro. Interesting approach; I have not heard of this before.

F: The developers found that mindset seems to have these three levels and each represents a very significant layer of what constitutes somebody's mindset. The first level is Meta Mindset, which is responsible for your big picture clarity. Your Meta Mindset relates to your fundamental attitude toward work, and where you think your place is in the world. As we discussed before, to help clarify and enrich each element of Meta Mindset, a well-known entrepreneur who typifies each aspect or quality of the Meta Mindset was selected to serve as a type of example. You will see their icons and will recognize them, I am sure.

One more key idea for the inventory is that your career, or the task of driving your team forward into the future, is very much like the journeys taken by the early explorers. They, too, needed to have a certain mindset and tools to arrive at their desired destinations, just like you do.

Assessing Meta Mindset – Big Picture Clarity

F: Are you ready to go through the Meta Mindset questions?

J: Sure.

F: The first question is about passion, which is about what gives you joy, what lights you up. John, what do you really love to do?

J: I don't know. I haven't thought about this for many years. I have always kind of thought that passion is an emotion and it shouldn't have all that much to do with business. As I think about it now, I guess I love building something new. I enjoy maintaining and sustaining a well-oiled machine less. I am excited about new ventures and projects, figuring out the next step, the next project, and getting it off the ground.

F: Great. It sounds like this area needs more exploration and you are not very clear on it. The statement here is, "I know what I really love to do and what I am passionate about." If you take a subjective scale of 0 to 10, where 10 means extremely clear and 0 means total uncertainty, what's your rating for this statement?

J: I guess I know what I love to do, but I also feel that I am not at all connected to it right now. I also think that I confuse passion and result orientation. I would actually give this a very low rate of 3.

F: Ok, noted. The key point here seems to be that if you want to enjoy what you do, you need to know your passion more clearly and then connect to it regularly. This is important as passion is the energy that keeps you going towards your goals. Now, let's go the second statement, which is, "I know what I want to help create in the longer-term future and am clear about my destination and longer-term vision."

Vision can best be defined as "a mental image of what the future will or could be like." The creative vision of a leader is about their ability to imagine and focus on longer-term possibilities that improve lives in some way. It involves the ability to see beyond the confines of the "here and now" and imagine future scenarios. It also involves the capacity to set and stay focused on longer-term goals, adopting long-term plans and a holistic view.

J: That one is very hard for me. I feel like I am very focused on what the current situation is in the company and how I am seemingly being "played out" by members of the senior management team. I really need to think about my longer-term future. When I think about that, I realize that I am more interested in creating and building new ventures than being an employee and managing a company.

F: I see; that's important to know. Like you mentioned regarding your passion, you seem to be all about building new things. Let me ask you, when you close your eyes and think about building something new, what do you see? What do you want to create in the world that is beyond you?

J: I see people using green energy everywhere. Businesses, homes, cities, and countries. I can see them from above, like a helicopter view. Yes, that's it. I would like to make the world a more sustainable place that relies on green energy. It sounds a bit too big, like I am bragging. I am very unclear on exactly what that future looks like and what the size of my achievement will be with respect to making the world greener.

F: Before you give me a rating for this one, let's talk about the third statement. It is, "I am clear about my direction, regardless of whether I know the ultimate destination." We differentiate between direction and destination for Vision exactly for the reasons you mentioned a minute ago. You might have a clear sense of the direction but not much clarity about the endgame, which is the destination, or vice versa. For some people, neither of these are clear. It sounds like you are saying that you are unclear about the destination but very clear on the direction. Is that fair?

J: Yes. I would say my destination clarity is like a 5 and the direction is pretty clear, so a 9.

F: Excellent. We can move to the fourth statement which is, "I know my purpose; I know what I stand for and why I am doing what I am doing." Again, a very important point for leadership, which relates to what Simon Sinek calls "the Why factor," our strongest motivator.

J: Again, I am at loss here. You are asking me pretty big and philosophical questions. Do people you work with tend to know their purpose?

F: I know it is a hard question. Most people struggle with it, but when I ask them some additional questions, it becomes clearer for them. Purpose helps us to keep going and find meaning and fulfillment in what we are doing. It is also very important in leadership, since our "golden circle" or purpose attracts others to come on the journey with us.

Let me ask you a few questions so we can determine the right rating here. One is, "What do you think you bring to the table when making your vision of a greener world happen?"

J: The ability to pull together a team and start a business?

F: Right. And what is your secret sauce? The special gifts, resources, or superpower that you bring to your team in order to make your vision happen?

J: Perhaps my strategic vision and planning skills; recruiting the right talent and structuring information in a convincing and inspirational manner.

F: Ok, so you are very unclear on the purpose you say, but it seems you have a better idea of what you bring to the table. In terms of a rating, what would you say this is?

J: Maybe a 6.

[Eventually, in Fred's work with John, coming up with the right purpose statement is a big AHA-moment for John. The statement is "I am a builder with a great commercial instinct to heal the environment."]

F: Great, the 6 is noted. Now, let's talk about the fifth statement about ambition. Ambition is a result of the desire and determination to achieve success and recognition for oneself. Ambition is defined as "a strong desire to do or to achieve something, typically requiring determination and hard work" that brings us personal benefit. Let me ask you a few questions around your ambition. The first is, "What type of life do you want to create for yourself?"

J: A life with more freedom. My own firm rather than being part of a large corporation where every minute of my time is controlled by someone else. I want to be in charge of my time and I want to blame only myself for any decision I take.

F: Ok, that's quite clear. And what would you say you want to accomplish? What type of status and performance make your heart pound?

J: I am a leader. I want to be a significant leader. I want a eulogy in the Economist. As a minimum, I want a CEO role rather than head of a division.

F: And what would you like to be recognized and/or remembered for in that eulogy? What would you like to be able to add to your resume or biography?

J: That I was an investor working with multiple businesses all aiming at the sustainability field.

F: Wow. That sounds very different from what you are doing now, doesn't it?

J: Yes. It has just hit me too. I think I need to leave this business in two years. Maybe my work here needs to focus on creating a great legacy, finding a successor, and building a strong team that can take over. Very interesting, I didn't think we would get to his place.

F: So, coming back to the statement, "I am clear about my ambition, i.e., what I want to become and achieve in the next two to five years."

J: Well, I think this is rather clear, though your questions have helped me a bit already. It's a 9 for me right now.

F: Excellent. This leads us to the sixth element of Meta Mindset, which is accountability and role clarity. Role is defined as "the function assumed, or part played, by a person in a particular situation." Thus, roles are related to both function, which is based upon competency, and the part played, which is determined by one's position or status. So, on the one hand, a role reflects personal skills, abilities, and effort, and on the other hand, it is about the position or relationship you have with co-workers, partners, competitors, and stakeholders. In fact, the statement for this is, "I am clear about my role, the position I have with respect to others in my market/environment."

I am curious how the insight regarding your ambition will help to answer this question. Do you know what type of person you need to become and what role you need to have to create the life you want, and succeed with your Ambition, Mission, and Vision?

J: Yes, I think I need to be more proactive and take things into my hands by paving my way out of this business while also setting up my team for success. I think I am seen as more of an outsider in the company, due to my different style and previous higher role. I also realize that I am a great mentor and starter, and less of a finisher. I think I will need more resilience, influencing, and team building competencies to build the legacy I would I like to leave.

So, I am pretty clear. That's a 9.

Assessing Macro Mindset – Habits of Success

F: Let's move to the second level of mindset, Macro Mindset. Your Macro Mindset relates to the mental disciplines and practices required to bring focus to the big picture, meta-level issues we have just discussed, and bring them into action. The macro level involves establishing habits of success, practices necessary for sustainable success. As you will see, these are certain qualities of mindset that manifest in effectively managing your energy and focus, seeking honest and frequent feedback, scanning for opportunities, dealing with risks and adversity, and recharging and balancing yourself. Macro Mindset helps you to know where to go and to stay on course.

The first statement is, "I am doing what I am passionate about and invest a lot of energy and focus into making what I want happen." While, on the meta level, it is important to be clear about your passion, on the macro level you need to consistently energize yourself and others by putting that passion into action and bringing focus to what you want.

J: Yes, there is a big disconnect for me on this one. I currently really don't invest much time in making my dream happen. I am constantly comparing my life to what it should be or could be or what others have achieved. I think this is a 4 for me.

F: Good insight. I think there is a clear thread here and, if you think about it, this is also something that people will pick up on. Your teams will notice that you passion, your heart, is not there. I get the feeling that this will have to be one of the key focus areas for our work.

It also leads us to the second statement here, which is about the *Seeker* Macro Mindset. "I seek feedback and have established ways to get honest and frequent feedback." How would you rate that?

J: Our company has certain mechanisms for feedback that are obligatory, and they relate to performance reviews, which we now call quarterly check-ins. But I guess you mean something else here?

F: Definitely. I mean your openness to feedback in general and your willingness to actively seek it – whether you have trusted people, mentors, or others who you use for getting regular feedback.

J: I would say that's a 5. I don't really have time or make time to do something like that. And I am also wondering a little bit whether reaching out like that is a sign of weakness. People in leadership positions must move forward and show strength. Asking for too much feedback could backfire, don't you think?

F: I don't know how you define "too much." I think the opposite is true. Seeking feedback is a sign of courage and openness, which not everyone has. For example, belonging to a great group of peers with rich experience in leadership, like a Mastermind circle, is extremely beneficial. You are all there to learn and support each other. Nobody will second guess why you are asking questions.

J: You might be right about that. I also realize that I haven't asked for feedback from my superiors for long time, thinking it should be obvious to them that I need it. As a result, I have made many assumptions and guesses about what they think of me and my work. I guess it is a matter of giving the right level of priority to these things and then making time and creating the right opportunity with the right people.

F: Very true. In fact, the third statement has to do with the *Scanner* mindset, which also relates to the previous areas. It states, "I am constantly scanning for opportunities and invest time to create them." The inventory uses the crow's nest of a sailing ship as a metaphor, signaling that it takes energy and curiosity to go up there and scan the horizon.

J: Right. From that perspective, I would say this is one of my areas of strength. I would give it a nine. I go to conferences, regularly reach out to a network of contacts, and am actively looking for opportunities all the time.

F: Great. This leads us to the next aspect of Macro Mindset, which is about recharging. In a very competitive corporate setting, we sometimes forget that if we don't take care of ourselves first, we won't have the chance to take care of others. Like they tell you on airplanes, bring the oxygen mask to yourself first and then put it on your children. The statement here reads, "I am internally grounded and resourceful and have my ways of recharging and balancing myself and practice them daily."

J: Another weakness. I think I am mad at myself. I am a bit of a slave driver and I keep telling myself, "I must do better." I realize that sounds terrible, but I think that's how I keep my motivation level up. Reminding myself not to be like my father, who got into trouble with law at the end. Anyway, that's another story, you are not my therapist.

F: Well, I think it is great that you had that insight and shared it with me. I get how it can be, in a strange sense, motivating to treat yourself like a slave, but I also think that it leads to burnout. And it probably makes you feel terrible. Also, if that's how you treat yourself, how do you treat others?

J: Very true. I give myself a 5.

F: Ok, noted. Finally, here is one that relates to the *Persister* Macro Mindset, which is about the ability to persevere when things are difficult. The statement is, "I am aware of risks and potential problems and don't get discouraged or distracted in the face of adversity and negative feedback."

J: I think that would be 9. I am pretty good at pushing myself and bouncing back. I keep saying to myself, "John, you've got this! How are you going to make this happen?" And, in the end, it always works out.

Assessing Micro Mindset – Ongoing Priorities

F: Ok. The third level of mindset is your Micro Mindset. This produces and guides the specific actions necessary to make your goals happen. Micro Mindset is like a spotlight that helps you prioritize on a daily level. For successful entrepreneurs and leaders, it is a function of identifying their ongoing priorities with respect to nine critical actions. The nine actions connect to the five core areas of what we call the "SFM Circle of Success," and they relate to self, customers, team, stakeholders, and partners. I will explain this more as we go through the inventory.

Some of the language you will hear is purposely related to entrepreneurship. In fact, I want to introduce the idea of *intrapreneurship* to you. The term "intrapreneur" is a blend of the two words "internal" and "entrepreneur," meaning someone who is an employee within a company but acts like an entrepreneur in charge of their own project or venture. In 1986, Steve Jobs was quoted in *Newsweek* as saying that the Macintosh team exhibited the qualities of intrapreneurship. In 2014, *Forbes* declared that the most valuable employees are the intrapreneurs. The idea is that there are certain projects that require the leadership of an "internal entrepreneur," like in the legendary creation of 3M or the Sony PlayStation. The term "intrapreneur" has since evolved into the idea of an employee or leader who has a truly entrepreneurial attitude, level of accountability, and inner drive. Thus, intrapreneurs take on the same qualities of mindset as entrepreneurs, especially Micro Mindset.

The MindsetMap uses a different system to evaluate Micro Mindset. Instead of rating statements on a scale of 1 to 10, it asks you to answer three things about activities related to building a Circle of Success: 1) Whether you like doing that activity. 2) Whether you think you are good at it. And 3) Whether you spend time doing it.

The first area of Micro Mindset, **SelfMotivator**, again has to do with passion, but this time, we are looking at it with the spotlight on a daily level. The statement here is about *"Setting aside the time to explore and reconnect with what I love to do, what is important to me, and what I am good at doing, i.e., my passion, my sense of purpose, and my excellence."* I am wondering, are you setting aside the time to explore and reconnect with what you love to do? For things that are important to you and what you are good at doing, things that fuel your purpose? As you do, consider whether reconnecting with your Passion is something you like doing, whether you are you good at it, and whether you actually spend time doing it.

J: I like it, certainly, but I am not good at it. I feel guilty doing things that I am passionate about. It feels selfish. For example, I love skiing, but when I do it alone, I almost always beat myself up about not doing it more with my wife and kids. And I don't make enough time for it. Also, there are many things at work that feel more purposeful for me, but I don't make time for them. I am too busy.

F: That's important to know and fits with a similar pattern in your Meta and Macro Mindsets. Let's get to the next step. I understand that you want to improve your connection to your passion and purpose which are to create new, purpose-driven ventures. Assuming you can reconnect to your passion and purpose the next step is that you want to bring this into the world. This requires the **MarketMaker** mindset and the need to connect with your customers. Are you "creating opportunities for ongoing dialog with customers and prospects?" Again, as you reflect on that activity, consider whether you like doing it, whether you are good at it, and whether you spend time doing it?

J: I think I am really good at this, I like it, and I do spend time doing it.

F: Great! This then leads us to the content of conversations with customers regarding the products and services you provide for them. Do you feel you put on your **ProductCreator** hat enough? Do you spend time "brainstorming, generating, and implementing products, solutions, and services that anticipate and fulfill customer needs?" Are you good at it? Do you like it?

J: Well, I am told I am good at this and I enjoy doing it. My role currently, the way it has evolved. doesn't allow me to do enough of this. But ultimately, I know I have time for what I make time for.

F: Ok, when was the last time you got this kind of feedback from someone – that you have formulated a new idea or solution personally or with your team? Do you have some recent positive feedback on that?

J: Yes, just yesterday one of our clients sent us an email thanking me and the team for figuring out how to creatively meet their needs. I always save this type of email and I have several that I can show you.

F: That sounds like good evidence. Since this is a self-rating exercise it is important that I check in with questions like that as to what evidence you have to support your ratings. This sounds like a well-founded rating.

That leads us to the TeamMaker mindset, which is about "attracting and providing direction and support to team members and encouraging team cooperation."

J: Again, I think I am good at it and I like it, but I don't spend enough time doing it.

F: Right. What do you think is the reason is for that? Why do you think you don't spend enough time doing it?

J: It has to do with my perception that we are always in a hurry and I have to devote more time to customers. Also, I get stuck in internal politics and find myself out of time for my people.

F: Ok, we can come back to this later. Remember the point about how people who are treating themselves poorly tend to do similarly with others? There maybe another pattern here.

J: Well, I guess I wouldn't go as far as to say that I am doing poorly. I would just say that I could do more for them.

F: Please don't take this as an attack. I think it is my role to show you some patterns. I just want to point out that if you don't have time for yourself it is also likely you don't have enough time for others. That's just the way it works. We can dig into this later. By the way, we call the next Micro Mindset the **CompetenceBuilder**, and it is about "encouraging and providing opportunities for team members to learn and grow." How are you doing in this area?

J: That's a strength for me. I would indicate all three positively. I like doing it, I am good at it, and I think I spend sufficient time doing it.

F: Well noted. So far, all these Micro Mindsets have had more to do with what we call the "soul" side of an individual. We are now going to dig into some that have to with the "ego" side. We believe that these two should be in balance and neither one should take more precedence than the other. When you put the two together, you have a balanced person who is both caring for others and decisive in key leadership moments. Are you ready for this?

J: Yes, that actually sounds very interesting; a new way of thinking of balance! Let's do it.

F: Awesome. Here is the first one, the FinanSourcerer. This is about "identifying potential investors and providers of other essential resources and creatively getting their interest and commitment to support your venture."

J: That's a strength for me. All three are a yes. I am good at it, I like it, and I spend time doing it.

F: Can you share a bit of your benchmark or evidence for these answers?

J: Surely. I have a very strong finance background and I spent some time working in corporate finance. I have also started my own company, managed to attract investors, and eventually sold it. In my current role I have the biggest budgets out of all of our subsidiaries. I actually enjoy doing this type of work a lot.

F: Thanks John, that sound quite solid. I have noted your answers. The next Micro Mindset, and you may notice that we sometimes call them hats, though some people want to wear these hats permanently, is called the VentureBuilder. This mindset focuses on "creating and developing a sustainable infrastructure and path for growth and scalability of your venture, project, or division."

J: Yes, that is another area where I am pretty strong by natural design. I also like it and I spend a lot of time on it.

F: Noted. The next one is the so-called **MatchMaker**, which has to do with "seeking and establishing win-win relationships with potential partners and allies who resonate with your values and vision."

J: I am beginning to enjoy this side a lot more than the first one. Again, that is something I am good at, I like it, and I spend time doing it.

F: Can you give some recent examples of that?

J: Sure. For example, I have recently established a strong connection with the green energy alliance, and we are just about to put together a conference in DC. I love doing projects like that.

F: Great. This takes us to the final "hat," which is the **ReSourcerer**. This mindset is all about "identifying and leveraging synergies between what you are doing and the products, services, or competencies of other ventures."

J: Same again. I am good at that, I like it, and I put a lot of time into it. I have to say that my ego side seems quite developed.

[Fred asks for some more specific evidence and examples of the ReSourcerer Micro Mindset and concludes that John has a solid basis for his answers. They then proceed to the final section of the inventory which is choosing the Meta Goal or current focus.]

Assessing Meta Goals – Current Focus

F: As a final step, I would like to ask you to think about your current focus which could be: 1) Increase my personal satisfaction in what I am doing, 2) Establish financial robustness/ stability, 3) Build a scalable business, 4) Make a genuine and meaningful contribution, or 5) Achieve greater innovation and resilience. Obviously, these focuses or Meta Goals are all very important. However, you cannot try to get all five at same time or you will be on a mission impossible, trying to eat a huge apple with one giant bite. That doesn't really work. In your current role, which out of the five is most important for you? What are you focusing on most in the next 12 months?

J: I believe the most important goal for me is building a scalable business. I believe that's what they expect of me and that's what I am currently focusing on.

F: I just want to pick up on the language you used here. You said, "that's what they expect of me," correct? That's all fine. What if you consider this question from another angle though? So, it's more like, what is most important for you right now as the leader of this team, applying the logic that you must first take care of your motivation level if you want to lead a highly motivated team that will create a scalable business?

J: I think there is clearly a pattern here that has to do with passion. I have clearly lost some of that in my current job. I am pushing myself to bring my best, but I have to really force it. It doesn't come with ease. I think if I could find more *personal satisfaction* in this role, I would be a better leader. But all this feels like a giant trap. I cannot really change how this position is set-up, so I am stuck.

F: I think you and I can work on a number things that will help you to find more satisfaction in this role, even if some of the external circumstance cannot be easily changed. Reconnecting with your passion and purpose is the best recipe, and it doesn't really depend on other people.

What does John's MindsetMap show?
The Success MindsetMaps Premium Report

The Success MindsetMap Inventory program automatically integrates all the pieces, Meta Mindset, Macro Mindset, Micro Mindset, and meta goals, with respect to the SFM Circle of Success and generates a 20-page *Premium Report* (shown in miniature below). The report reviews the details of the coachee's answers and summarizes the coachee's MindsetMap in a diagram, which is then contrasted with the ideal mindset that is most effective to achieve the selected focus or Meta Goal. Recommendations are then made regarding tools and processes that can be used by the coach and coachee to improve the needed areas of Meta, Macro and Micro Mindset.

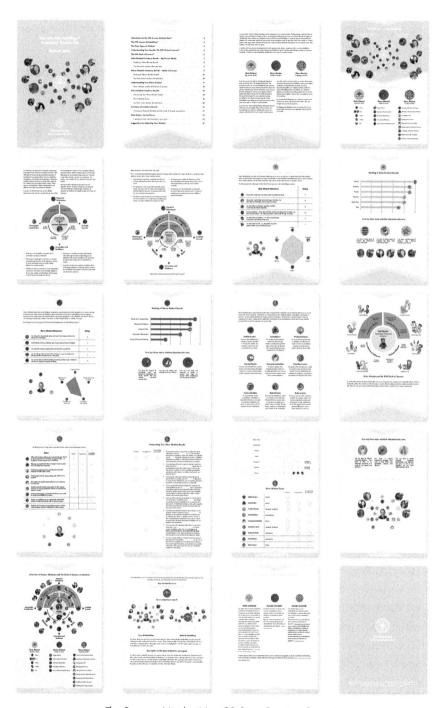

The Success MindsetMap 20-Page Premium Report

We often encourage MindsetMap coaches to start by reviewing the overall summary with their coachees. One great contribution of Success MindsetMap is its ability to show a person's current mindset in a single image. Below is the map of John's current mindset that emerged as a result of his sessions with Fred. The strength and brightness of the color of the icons indicates the strength of the rating that has been given to that aspect of mindset.

Map of John's current mindset

We can see right away that, at the level of Meta Mindset, John has the sense of direction of Anita Roddick, the ambition of Steve Jobs, and the clarity of role of Howard Schultz. These qualities are mirrored by the three explorers Christopher Columbus, Sir Francis Drake, and Admiral Horatio Nelson. John is weaker with the Meta Mindset qualities of vision/destination and purpose/mission and has very little spark of passion for what he is doing.

At the level of Macro Mindset, John's strengths are scanning for opportunities and persisting in the face of adversity. He is weaker in the areas of seeking frequent and honest feedback and recharging and balancing himself. However, he lacks much energy and focus for what he is doing.

John has strengths in many areas of Micro Mindset. His areas for improvement are SelfMotivator, TeamMaker, and ProductCreator.

When we see all the levels and aspects of mindset as a whole, it is a bit like seeing the pieces of a jigsaw puzzle coming together, and key patterns often become more obvious.

Perhaps the most important part of the Success MindsetMap Inventory is its ability to show which levels and areas of mindset are most important to strengthen or enhance to achieve the coachee's current focus for their project or venture. The MindsetMaps Inventory program compares the coachee's current mindset with the ideal mindset needed to reach a particular meta goal and indicates areas for improvement with a red circle around the relevant icon.

John initially identified his current focus as *building a scalable business*. With some coaching from Fred, John realized that his actual current focus needed to be *achieving greater personal satisfaction* in what he was doing.

Had John stayed with "building a scalable business," his comparison report would have looked like the below. The red circles show the key areas for improvement.

Your MindsetMap   Ideal MindsetMap

John's Meta Mindset and Micro Mindset were already completely attuned to achieving that outcome. He would have needed to work on the two areas of Macro Mindset of bringing much more energy and focus to what he was doing and seeking frequent and honest feedback.

When John realized that his current focus really needed to be *increasing personal satisfaction* in what he was doing, his comparison report showed a quite different set of areas for him to work on (with some overlap), as seen in the below diagram. Work was needed at every level of Mindset, Meta, Macro, and Micro.

Your MindsetMap   Ideal MindsetMap

As we can see on the above map, to increase personal satisfaction in what he is doing, John would need to adopt a Meta Mindset more like Richard Branson of the Virgin Group. This would mean to "follow his passions – in a way that served the world and himself." He would also need to have a "lust for adventure" like the mythical traveler Ulysses and feel the desire "to strive, to seek, to find and not to yield."

In fact, John's current mindset was ideally oriented for the Meta Goal of *achieving financial robustness and stability*. He had great Micro Mindset abilities as FinanSourcerer and MarketMaker to support his strong ambition, along with the Macro Mindset qualities of scanning for opportunities and persisting in the face of adversity. The challenge, however, was that he couldn't play this role authentically. People didn't feel the spark in him, nor did he feel it in himself.

The Mindset Changes Required in John's Case

If we shift to look at the specific rankings of Meta Mindset results provided by the Success MindsetMaps *Premium Report*, some of the mindset adjustments John needs to make become obvious.

Ranking of Meta Mindset Results

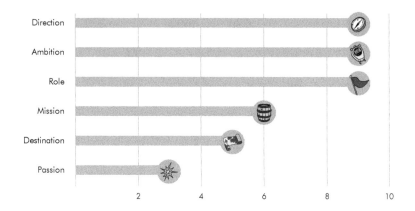

It is clear that John needed to increase his ability to be in touch with the *spark* that would come from connecting with his passion. The coaching session with Fred also established that the vision John had for his longer-term *direction* lay outside of the organization he was currently working for, and that he could not really live his passion of starting new projects and ventures in this current role. This was a big step forward. On the other hand, it presented a major challenge about how he should proceed and feel about his current role.

The *Premium Report's* presentation of John's Macro Mindset results also showed a clear imbalance in John's current mindset.

Ranking of Macro Mindset Results

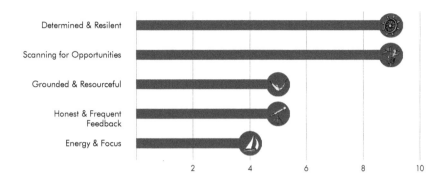

As a result of the coaching session with Fred, John realized he would need greater energy and focus and to go "full sail" for what he wanted. However, in this particular case, it was not possible, given the constraints of his role.

Another important area of change was related to bringing John into his "zone of genius" with respect to key aspects of Micro Mindset. An important prerequisite for this, as we know, is that to be a genius in any area of Micro Mindset, minimally all three options need to be checked (I like it, I am good at it, I spend time doing it) and there has to be a rating of 8 or above for Passion, Vision, or Ambition, depending on which aspect of Micro Mindset is being addressed.

- If the user doesn't have a rating of 8 or above for passion, vision, or ambition, they will not have any areas of genius.

- For TeamMaker or CompetenceBuilder to be a zone of genius, the Meta Mindset area of Purposeful/Mission must be rated 8 or higher.

- Similarly, for MatchMaker or ReSourcerer to be a zone of genius, the Meta Mindset area of Accountable/Role must be rated 8 or higher.

The *Success MindsetMaps Inventory Premium Report* results for John's Micro Mindset were as follows:

		I enjoy it	I'm good at it	I'm spending time doing it
	SelfMotivator	untapped excellence			
	TeamMaker	untapped excellence			
	ProductCreator	untapped excellence			
	MarketMaker	excellence			
	CompetenceBuilder	excellence			
	FinanSourcerer:	excellence			
	VentureBuilder	excellence			
	MatchMaker	excellence			
	ReSourcerer	excellence			

Micro Mindset Zones

These report results make it clear that John is a highly competent individual with a level of excellence in many parts of building a Circle of Success. There is no level of genius, however, which is what is needed for John to move to the next level of what he wants in his life and his career. He would also need to be able to reach at least a level of excellence in some other areas to succeed in his current focus.

Reflecting on these results from the Success MindsetMaps Premium Report, below is how the next part of the conversation took place between John and Fred.

F: So, let's look at this together. What do you notice when you look at this Micro Mindset zone chart?

J: Well, first, I can see I have a lot of self-confidence. Joking aside, I notice that I have a lot of excellence, but it's clear that I don't have any genius. (Smiling) I am sure you will tell me what that means. Also, that I need to spend more time in the areas of SelfMotivator, TeamMaker, and ProductCreator.

F: Well, let's talk about the meaning of zones. When you are good at something, like it, and spend time doing it, you are in the zone of excellence. One level down from that would be when you are good at something, and you spend time doing it; that's a competence. Genius is when, in addition to the three checked criteria, you have an 8 or higher rate for your Vision, Mission, and Ambition. In other words, your excellence is in service of making your Vision happen, so that you can fulfil your Mission and achieve your goals. In your case, your Ambition was rated high, but you had lower scores for your Passion and Mission of 3 and 6, respectively.

J: Wow, this is so true. I feel like I am doing a really good job, but somehow, it's neither exciting nor really fulfilling for me. I have got to fix the passion and mission problem to get to my genius. That really resonates with me.

Next Steps and Results

As we have pointed out before, all of the key mindset shifts John needed to make would be difficult to impossible to do within the confines of his current role and company. However, by Fred helping John to clarify his passion and longer-term vision, which was clearly outside the company, John paradoxically regained his strength and motivation to make the changes happen that he needed to succeed within his current company context. As he was able to see his future more clearly, John realized that he needed to find his successor and coach them to be able to take over from him in ten to twelve months, and he was willing to make some tougher decisions he had been hesitating about for a while.

As often happens, John also found that he needed to develop more of the means and discipline to take care of and recharge himself and not become overly stressed or burned out. To do that, he needed to set aside more time to explore and reconnect with what he loved to do, what was important to him, and what he was good at doing, i.e., his Passion, his sense of purpose, and his excellence.

The key issue for John was that he needed to see his future more clearly. As a result of going through the *Success MindsetMaps Inventory*:

- John realized that he was neither connected to his Passion (Passionate) nor clear on his Mission (Purposeful).

- Once he was clearer on his Passion and Mission, John decided that he needed to select and train his successor so he could move on the next level in his life and career.

- John, with Fred's help, identified his successor and began to focus more on his team.

As a follow up to the coaching session with John, Fred and John had John's team take the *Success MindsetMaps Team Inventory* (see Chapter 12). This allowed them to identify multiple challenges from a team leadership point of view.

- First, the team had no shared Vision. It was unclear what results and objectives they wanted to reach in the longer-term future. They had annual individual objectives, but they did not share those with each other.

- Given that they only had individual goals, they had not discussed what the interdependencies were and what were their common goals as a team.

- There was no clear mission statement for the team. All this resulted in very little cooperation and high levels of competitiveness amongst the team members.

- John, the team leader, was demotivated and couldn't be a positive example of a highly spirited, effective, innovative team member, which is what he expected from others on the team.

Once this was clear, Fred and John were able build a development process for John's team, which included:

a. Defining the team Vision and Mission.

b. Connecting company values to their Vision.

c. Discussing Vision/Mission/Ambition and setting objectives in accordance with the vision.

d.   Discussing roles and key competencies.

e.   Developing competence and introducing an ongoing on-the-job coaching system.

f.   Developing a best practice sharing process.

Fred's intervention was a major success for John, his team, and their company. The MindsetMaps Inventory was the "difference that made the difference," in John's opinion. He claimed that the MindsetMaps coaching process really produced the spark he needed to propel both the organization and his career forward. He cited the courage of the process and how very personal questions were addressed which would normally be considered off-limits. The trust he built with Fred during this process continued to last through the entire intervention. So much so that John also sought out additional personal advice and follow-ups from Fred as he engaged with his team and his chosen successor and, later, moved on to the next stage in his life and career.

INTRAPRENEURSHIP AND THE MINDSETMAP TEAM REPORT

In parallel with the idea of the next-generation entrepreneur we have been exploring in this book, the business world has seen the rise of another trend, that of the intrapreneur. The term "intrapreneur" is a blend of the two words "internal" and "entrepreneur." It was first coined by Gifford Pinchot III and Elizabeth S. Pinchot in a 1978 white paper titled *Intra-Corporate Entrepreneurship* for the Tarrytown School for Entrepreneurs. In 1986, Steve Jobs was quoted in *Newsweek* as saying that the Macintosh team exhibited the qualities of intrapreneurship. In 2014, *Forbes* declared that the most valuable employees are intrapreneurs. The idea was that there are certain projects that require the leadership of an "internal entrepreneur," like the legendary creation of 3M or the Sony PlayStation.

The term "intrapreneur" has since evolved into the idea of an employee or leader who has an entrepreneurial attitude and mindset, a high level of accountability, and inner drive. The concept gained further traction with the Covid19 pandemic when employees needed to become independent "intrapreneurs" overnight. Following the pandemic, many people still work from home or are in a hybrid arrangement and are under less direct in-person supervision. This creates the need for employees to be more self-motivated and disciplined and to be given more freedom and empowerment than ever before. All this points to a new mindset that is necessary for both employees and those who lead them.

As an example, one of our clients has built a very successful company from scratch. Seven years ago, he and his partner worked from home. Today, they have several hundred employees and are one of the leading brands in their sector, with revenues of hundreds of millions of dollars. The company seems unstoppable, and yet, the client's biggest worry remains his employees' mindset. He complains that most people on his team are reactive, magnify negatives, and don't look for solutions independently. In our coaching sessions, he often wonders how he could get them to be more like internal entrepreneurs rather than employees. He wants a team of intrapreneurs who care for the business as if it was their own and are motivated to go the extra mile. This leads to the question, "What is the mindset of a successful intrapreneur like?"

We know there is much resonance between an entrepreneur and an intrapreneur. An entrepreneur starts and owns a venture as a means of providing goods or services to customers and must build a Circle of Success. Similarly, an intrapreneur works inside an organization with multiple internal and external stakeholders, develops services or solutions, explores policies and technologies, builds teams, and forms partnerships that will help improve the performance of the organization. As such, an intrapreneur needs to develop skills and competencies that are very like those of an entrepreneur. No doubt, all employers would love to see their employees acting like owners of their businesses as opposed to passive followers or paid contributors.

Both entrepreneurs and intrapreneurs need to build a Circle of Success. Consider the example of a world-famous wildlife photographer and entrepreneur Mickey recently interviewed. This man had been passionate about wildlife and wild animals from childhood. This passion eventually led to a calling to do something about preserving wildlife and biodiversity, which originated in a personal experience of seeing a wild animal killed. The calling became his purpose, to express the love and passion he felt for these animals and do something tangible by educating people and taking steps to protect them. He had a vision of a world where people live in a rediscovered connection to animals and plants and adapt protocols and laws to protect endangered species. He connected his Passion and Vision to his excellence and genius, which was a particularly emotional style of wildlife photography. His approach includes spending intimate time with animals in the wilderness, sometimes living with them for days at a time to capture their life in a truly authentic way. All this culminated in awareness of his Mission and career to bring these powerful photos to the world and reconnect humans to animals and nature.

The photographer quickly evolved from being a lonely artist to an inspirational activist who attracted a team around him. The team's Ambition to make visible differences with respect to the Mission to protect endangered species led to the need to scale the business and develop a set of products built around the idea of promoting biodiversity. The team also started seeking and getting grants and financial support for conservation initiatives. Their vision and unique contribution in the form of a signature photo style attracted other partners who shared their values, and the power of the effort was multiplied.

This example illustrates how the photographer was able to go from being a lone wolf to gathering a pack of wolves by applying the powerful building blocks of Meta Mindset, namely Passion, Vision, Mission/Purpose, Ambition, and Role. How does this relate to a leader in an organization? A leader can be likened to a captain of a ship. They also need to find the right crew and convince them to board the ship and join them on their journey. This takes passion, purpose, and clarity of vision. A captain needs to share their vision and purpose and convince all crewmembers onboard to bring their best to accomplish the common mission.

That includes selecting and then developing the team members and giving them a sense of progress and purpose. A leader also needs to have clarity on what ambition and success look like for themselves personally, as well as for the team. They need to know the specific goals they want to achieve within a set timeframe. Then, they need to formulate a plan for how they will influence all the stakeholders involved who could either support or block their success. The journey is tough, so mental discipline on the Macro Mindset level is crucial along the way. Finally, leaders need to get their priorities right daily, which is driven by their Micro Mindset, to balance many different types of people and roles on the team as well as in their own mindset. For instance, there will be contexts when a leader needs to wear a MarketMaker, CompetenceBuilder, FinanSourcerer, or MatchMaker, hat, etc. The outer game or business context of an entrepreneur may be very different from the everyday realities of an intrapreneur within an organization. The inner game or mindset needed to succeed, however, is surprisingly similar. Thus, the core components of an intrapreneur's Meta, Macro, and Micro Mindset are essentially the same as those of a successful entrepreneur.

If you are a coach who works with conscious leaders or those who strive to become one, the MindsetMaps Inventory provides a great way to bring the conversation to the key success factors which matter most for achieving the goal a leader has selected.

THE MINDSETMAPS TEAM REPORT

The twenty-eight-page *MindsetMaps Team Report* is a powerful addition to the MindsetMaps Inventory that has been designed to work with a team and visualize the team mindset. The team mindset explored in the report is the collective inner attitude of a team as they set out to achieve specific Meta Goals. We ask all team members to take the inventory as individuals in their respective roles. Then, we combine their results to see how aligned the team is and where they are on their collective journey to their goal. The results illuminate the Meta, Macro, and Micro levels of their collective attitude and indicate which vital critical competencies are necessary for the team to attain success.

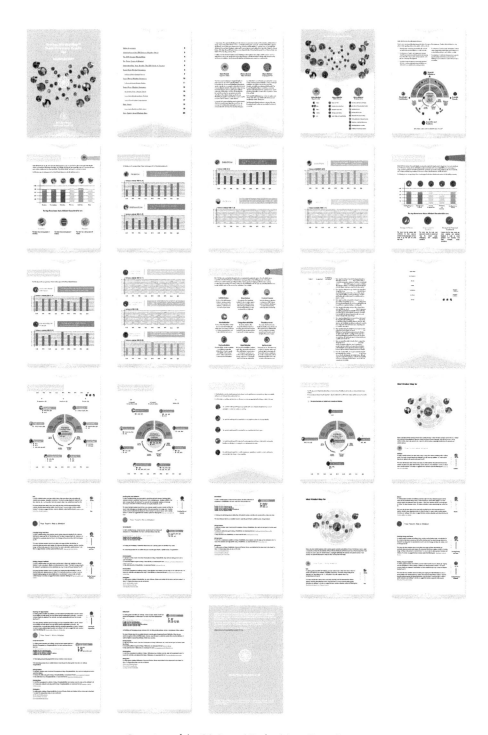

Overview of the 28-Page MindsetMaps Team Report

In this chapter, we want to share a specific case to show you how the team report can be applied to organizational development work. However, first, we would like to share some methodological considerations and explain why we build the team report the way we do.

When we set out to create the MindsetMaps Team Report, there were many questions to answer, including:

- Should a team member fill out the inventory for the team or for themselves? In other words, is the question about "we" or "me"?

- What is the nature of a team mindset? Is it meaningful to say, "We are clear about our vision," or "We are not so clear about our ambition"?

- Should we ask people for a self-assessment, or should they also rate each other?

Our conclusion was that we are generally ineffective judges of others and "us as a team," but we can be more reliable judges of ourselves with a coach who asks for examples and evidence and helps us calibrate our use of the rating scale. There is a growing volume of research supporting that 360° type assessments are not accurate but that people can reliably self-assess when given sufficient help. When we get better data from everyone, it will make sense when we combine it, as opposed to trying to get the team members to rate each other, which is always more about personal opinions and generalizations than objective data. For example, by combining the results of individual self-assessments, we can reach meaningful conclusions like "we have a lot of people with a clear vision in this team," which will also mean that the team itself is likely to have a good sense of vision, they just need to align on it. At that point, it is a meaningful next step for a leader or facilitator to ask team members to state their vision to see how aligned they are. The team coach, for instance, may also conclude that not many on the team have a sense of mission, which will make it very hard for them to operate as a "mission-driven team." In such a situation, the MindsetMaps Team Report will point to a clear diagnosis and set of interventions for developing a sense of a common mission for the team that can be implemented with the help of a MindsetMaps certified coach.

APPLYING THE MINDSETMAP TEAM REPORT – A CASE STUDY

An example of how the MindsetMap Team Report can be applied is provided by the work Mickey did with the leadership team of a Fortune 500 company. His assignment was to support the CEO in strengthening his team so they could successfully lead the company through a key organizational transformation. Mickey first explained to the CEO that "strengthening the team" should start with strengthening and aligning their mindsets as the most crucial foundation for getting to their goals and outcomes. From there, it was easy to explain why they should look at both the individual and team level mindsets and Meta Goals for diagnostic purposes and use the MindsetMaps Inventory for that.

The Beginning – Working with the CEO's Individual Report

When the CEO did his individual MindsetMaps Inventory as part of the diagnostic and preparatory phase, he selected *Increasing Innovation and Resilience* as his Meta Goal. The chart below shows the gap analysis chart in the CEO's MindsetMaps Premium Report.

Your Current Focus is:

Achieve greater innovation and resilience.

Your comparison report:

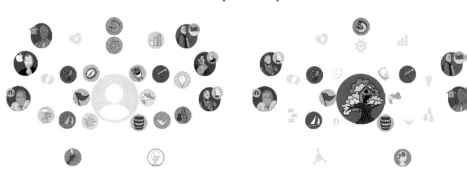

Your MindsetMap   **Ideal MindsetMap**

This chart shows a generally strong Meta Mindset, but with lower levels of Passion and Direction. Seeing this, the CEO realized that he had been living with a very strong sense of duty and purpose but found little joy in what he was doing. According to the MindsetMap, the two most important Meta Mindset qualities that are key to achieving the chosen goal of more innovation and resilience are being purposeful (having a mission) and being Accountable (clear on Role). When viewing the results, we always first consider those Meta Mindset areas for development, as they are connected to the pattern of the ideal mindset for the Meta Goal. In this case, we can see that, for the CEO, Mission and Role are both strong, since the red flag and cargo barrel icons appear in full color on the map.

In most cases, if we find that the Meta level is supportive of the goal, we move to examine Macro Mindset. On the other hand, it is also important to consider that Meta Mindset is foundational for all aspects of the Circle of Success, and if someone doesn't have passion, they won't have energy, except maybe out of a sense of duty. Duty frequently comes with extra effort and grinding teeth. Running continually on extra effort will likely end up bringing someone close to burnout. This was especially true in the case of this CEO since his Macro Mindset ratings showed that he didn't spend enough time recharging and balancing. His ratings also showed low scores for the key Macro Mindset quality of Energizer, which relates to investing energy and focusing on the right priorities, necessary qualities for achieving innovation and resilience. The CEO's lack of connection to Passion and energy also showed up on the level Micro Mindset, where it was evident that he lacked ongoing activities that brought him motivation and joy beyond just a sense of purpose. Interestingly, these patterns in the CEO's mindset were exacerbated by the fact that he led a team of technocrats who also had a lot of ambition and perseverance but with less focus on recharging and balancing.

Additionally, the two Micro Mindsets that are crucial for the CEO's chosen Meta Goal of greater innovation and resilience are Resourcerer and CompetenceBuilder. He rated both of these at a low level; Resourcerer was only a hobby, and CompetenceBuilder was just an interest (as you can see on the following chart from the CEO's Premium Report).

Micro Mindset Zones

		I enjoy it	I'm good at it	I'm spending time doing it
SelfMotivator	interest	○		
TeamMaker	excellence	○	○	○
ProductCreator	untapped excellence	○	○	
MarketMaker	interest	○		
CompetenceBuilder	interest	○		
FinanSourcerer:	competence		○	○
VentureBuilder	hobby	○		○
MatchMaker	excellence	○	○	○
ReSourcerer	hobby	○		○

Another key indication on this chart was that the CEO did not operate in the zone of genius for any area of Micro Mindset. This had to do with his lower level of Passion and lack of clarity on Direction. Reflecting on these diagnostic results led to a personal breakthrough for the CEO regarding the need to reset his mindset to find more passion and regularly reconnect with it.

Integrating the MindsetMaps Team Report
– Meta Mindset Sets the Stage

Using the MindsetMaps Team Report, Mickey was then able to analyze the CEO's individual results in light of the results from the rest of his team. In this case, the Meta Goal for the team was also greater innovation and resilience. The below diagram provides an overview of the ideal mindset for that goal and how the team scored for the key aspects of Meta, Macro, and Micro Mindset.

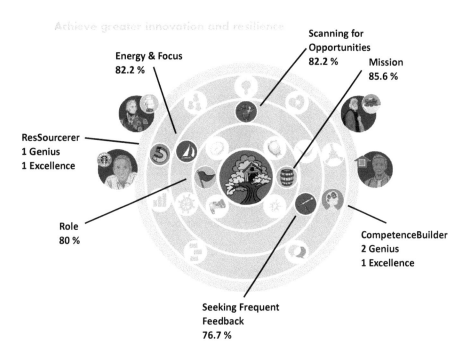

At first sight, these results seem hopeful in the sense that the team rating was pretty much at 80% for all key mindset aspects that are important for achieving greater innovation and resilience. However, although 80% is good, it could be better, and it is certainly not yet in the zone of genius, which was the aim and desire of this team. Also, sometimes identifying areas for growth requires a more careful analysis of the Meta, Macro, and Micro level results in general and beyond any particular Meta Goal. For instance, the following chart shows the team's Meta Mindset results:

Meta Mindset has to do with our fundamental attitude toward our work, our world and our place in that world. Meta Mindset relates to success factors at the levels of **purpose and identity.** Our Meta Mindset is essentially made up of our sense of passion, vision, mission, ambition and role. These provide the **"big-picture clarity"** with regard to our project or venture.

The following were the ratings given for the Meta Mindset statements on the MindsetMaps inventory:

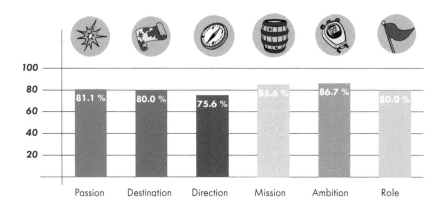

Team Meta Mindset Summary

There is good news but also some challenges with respect to these ratings. On the one hand, the team was quite passionate, which helped to balance the CEO's lower level of Passion and energy. On the other hand, we see there was a need to create more clarity regarding Direction, which was not easy when the CEO himself lacked clarity. Also, the high level of Ambition and sense of Mission combined with a less clear Direction made for a team where individuals were charging to meet their own passions and goals but had less clarity about their Roles. As a result of this more ego-driven and ambitious attitude, combined with professional silos, there were few synergies emerging in this team, according to their self-assessment. People were passionate about their goals but found it hard to resonate together, which limited the degree of collective intelligence they could apply.

The Team Report results provided a good "aha-moment" about that for the team, and Mickey helped the team clarify their direction and role more clearly, both on team and individual levels. The conversations regarding the key elements of Meta Mindset provided the basis for a profound paradigm shift for the team. They became united by a new sense of vision and role. They moved from seeing themselves in a support position to being more in the role of trailblazing leadership. Since this shift affected the highest levels of change, like purpose, identity, and core beliefs, it also brought a new set of behaviors and activated previously underutilized capabilities. Mickey helped the team identify specific business contexts and areas where innovation and resilience were needed and established measurable objectives and KPIs that allowed the team to monitor whether they were on the right track for their new direction and role. These objectives ranged from initiating specific actions to establishing new policies and achieving certain results by taking a stronger stance in key decision meetings.

The Team's Macro Mindset Determines Sustainability

At the level of Macro Mindset, the team's high ambitions had previously resulted in the team members being constantly in overdrive with little attention to what really mattered to each individual or on recharging and getting frequent, high-quality feedback. This was an interesting mirroring of the CEO's individual Macro Mindset. Perhaps not surprisingly, it is often the case that a leader's mindset heavily influences the mindset of their team members. The following chart shows the Team Report for Macro Mindset:

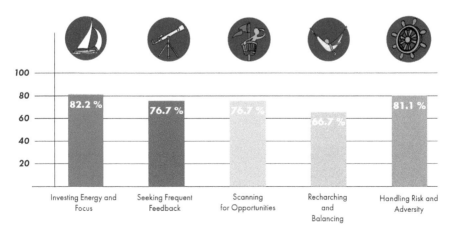

Reflecting on these results with Mickey's support triggered another deep discussion for the team members about the danger of burnout. Several new individual and team habits were identified to create more sustainability. These habits and decisions were related to clarifying boundaries for communications, sometimes as simple as when and how quickly team members should respond to emails or be available for phone calls and meetings over weekends and holidays. With Mickey's help, a new level of "public commitment" was reached that helped the team to establish "guard rails." The updated Macro Mindset habits created new pathways for more feedback and prioritizing the investment of energy and focus into activities based on the commitments, and team members stated what activities they truly enjoyed and believed to be most important. Achieving alignment with respect to these priorities was transformational since these agreements involved issues that Steven Covey calls "important but not urgent" and therefore are often underprioritized, like (self-) motivation and strategic planning. These issues also relate to key Micro Mindset priorities, like developing competencies of team members, which are crucial for achieving the team's goal of greater innovation and resilience.

The Team's Collective Micro Mindset is the Final Key to Success

The MindsetMaps Team Report shows the collective Micro Mindset strengths and weaknesses of the team. We often refer to this part of the report as the answer to the question, "Who is at the table?" In fact, a good metaphor for the SFM Circle of Success is a round table where all nine Micro Mindset competencies, like knights around King Arthur's round table, need to congregate if the team is to achieve its Meta Goal. In a high-performing team, all individuals are aware of all nine competencies and prepared to engage them when needed at various stages of building a Circle of Success. The MindsetMaps Team Report shows the team members around the "table" with their geniuses, excellences, and competencies. Significant areas are often empty, which is where another part of the report, the "opportunity chart," comes in handy. There may be people on the team who, with sufficient clarification and coaching support, can step into the empty areas and fill in the gaps.

In the case of the team Mickey was coaching, we can see that the area of CompetenceBuilder only had one team member with excellence, and that of ReSourcerer was empty. The good news was that the "untapped potential" chart on the left showed that there were team members for both areas who could start engaging in those competencies more often. These were particularly important Micro Mindsets since the team had chosen more innovation and resilience as their Meta Goal.

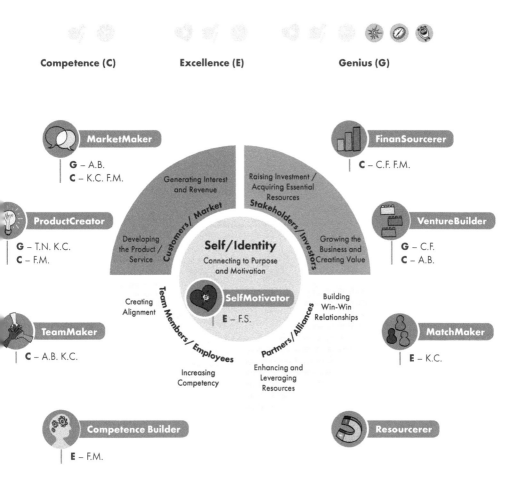

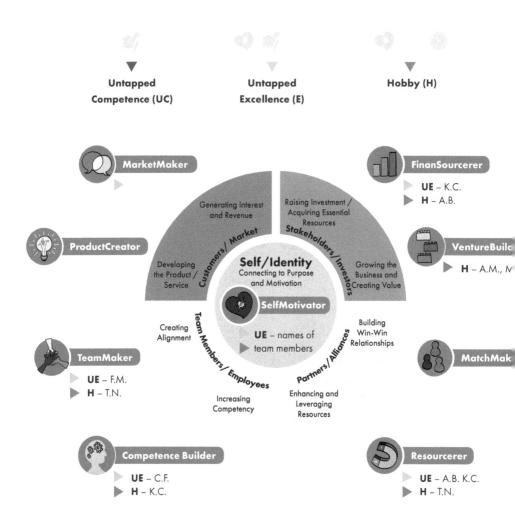

Untapped
Competence (UC)

Untapped
Excellence (E)

Hobby (H)

MarketMaker

FinanSourcerer
UE – K.C.
H – A.B.

ProductCreator

VentureBuild
H – A.M., M

Generating Interest
and Revenue

Raising Investment /
Acquiring Essential
Resources

Stakeholders/Investors

Customers/ Market

Self/Identity
Connecting to Purpose
and Motivation

Developing
the Product /
Service

Growing the
Business and
Creating Value

SelfMotivator

UE – names of
team members

Building
Win-Win
Relationships

Creating
Alignment

Team Members/ Employees

Partners/ Alliances

TeamMaker
UE – F.M.
H – T.N.

MatchMak

Increasing
Competency

Enhancing and
Leveraging
Resources

Competence Builder
UE – C.F.
H – K.C.

Resourcerer
UE – A.B. K.C.
H – T.N.

Guiding the team to reflect on these results, Mickey found that other team members were reluctant to engage the competencies related to their understanding of their roles and thus their priorities. Once the team defined "competence development" and "finding synergies" as their top priorities, it shifted the Micro Mindset of those team members with potential in these two areas to become more active. Furthermore, all team members realized that they needed to make more time to develop their abilities as CompetenceBuilder and ReSourcerer.

CONCLUSION – MINDSET MATTERS MOST

In summary, the combination of the individual and team MindsetMap reports provided the opportunity for all team members to become more mindful intrapreneurs. They all reflected on their individual results with Mickey before getting together for a workshop to better align their team mindset. At the workshop, they made progress on strengthening key areas of Meta, Macro, and Micro Mindset for their common success and set individual and team goals and actions to achieve more innovation and resilience. The MindsetMaps Inventory and Team Report served as vehicles for more self-awareness and created more understanding for each person with respect to their coworkers. They reconnected with a compelling individual and collective vision and sense of role that led to more sustainable success. The power of the MindsetMaps approach and the MindsetMaps Team Report is that it shifts attention and conversation to areas that otherwise might not come up if a team is left to a more open-ended process. Knowing what matters for different Meta Goals saves a tremendous amount of time and makes these conversations and interventions much more effective.

CLOSING
REFLECTIONS

We, executive coaches, leadership trainers, human resources or employee experience professionals, and leaders, all work in a business context. The Success MindsetMap Inventory was designed to fit this context and help transform it. We believe that this business context has evolved in a more conscious direction. Consciousness, in this sense, can be described as "an increased interest for the system that businesses are part of, like communities, countries, and sectors, and the environment on a larger scale." This systemic awareness has also led to a shift for many businesses and corporations to be more purpose-driven. Purpose may be defined as "an intention to make a positive difference in the world and respond to some of the critical challenges facing humanity." Using our terminology, we call this a global Meta and Macro Mindset shift. These businesses and leaders are interested in contributing and creating value, not only for their shareholders and customers but also for their staff and the society to which they belong. To illustrate how much of a Meta Mindset shift we are talking about, here is how, only fifty-two years ago, on September 13, 1970, Milton Friedman, a leading economic mind of his age, started his article in *The New York Times Magazine*:

> "When I hear businessmen speak eloquently about the "social responsibilities of business in a free-enterprise system, ...
> The businessmen believe that they are defending free enterprise when they declaim that business is not concerned "merely" with profit but also with promoting desirable "social" ends; that business has a "social conscience" and takes seriously its responsibilities for providing employment, eliminating discrimination, avoiding pollution and whatever else may be the catchwords of the contemporary crop of reformers. ... Businessmen who talk this way are unwitting puppets of the intellectual forces that have been undermining the basis of a free society these past decades."

Reading his lines, it is evident that he saw only two types of meta goals for business at the time, those related to financial robustness and profitability and growth related to scaling a business. Our research into successful leadership and business conduct has shown how setting clear meta goals and focuses like meaningful contribution, increased motivation and satisfaction at work, and innovation and resilience require a different mindset and lead to very different decisions and actions. We have shared with you the connections between mindset levels and meta goals in the various case studies in this book.

As we speak to corporate leaders worldwide, we find that many of them have heard about conscious business conduct and conscious leadership, and there is a growing interest in being part of this "movement." We also regularly hear them describing the need for new tools to facilitate greater mindset change. We have responded to the needs expressed by these leaders wanting to make more mindset shift by creating the Success MindsetMaps Inventory, web application, and coaching process.

We did that because we saw how, for decades, the narrow focus on the Meta Goal of profitability only shaped corporate America and the rest of the world through leadership practices and management education. Interestingly, there were several missed opportunities. For example, the financial crisis of 2008-2009 was a moment of possible awakening, but it was quickly subdued, and corporations went back to their original practices. In looking for a mindset-level explanation of why these potential historic opportunities didn't bring about more change, we have found that the three levels of mindset are crucial to get us moving into sustainable action. Real change only happens when a particular set of Meta, Macro, and Micro Mindsets are present. It seems to us that up until now, we have missed significant elements of that. The key stakeholders involved in corporate and legislative governance have missed a compelling vision set in harmony with concrete ambition and a clear timeline. Beyond the meta-level clarity, the Macro and Micro Mindset identities and qualities influence daily what priorities will be set and acted on instead of procrastinating, delaying, or avoiding. Micro Mindset directs people's attention spotlight and determines their daily habits.

Yet, the global Meta Mindset shift continues. For example, in 2019, 200 chief executives, including the leaders of Apple, Pepsi, and Walmart, all part of the so-called Business Roundtable, issued a statement on "the purpose of a corporation," arguing that companies should no longer advance only the interests of shareholders. Instead, the group said, they must also invest in their employees, protect the environment and deal fairly and ethically with their suppliers.

Few events have had such a compounded impact on humanity and business as the Covid 19 pandemic of 2020-2022. One such influence is the significant change in how corporations have pursued their social agenda and led their staff. Companies have become more open to hybrid working models, where employees only have to spend a certain amount of time in the office and can work some days from home. This provides time savings and more balance for many working parents and commuters in general. There is more awareness of mental health at work and more discussion of engagement and inspirational culture. Employees working from home also exemplify how "intrapreneurship" has become a key factor and how team members in this environment need a different type of (self-) leadership as well as (self-) motivation. Hence, the relevance of Macro Mindset qualities, like energy, focus, balance, and resilience connected to self-management has significantly increased. These Macro Mindset qualities are also essential to both individual and team sustainability. One of the key patterns we have seen in our research is how leaders who can energize others and seek feedback as they scan for new opportunities are much more successful in recharging themselves and their teams. They are also more successful in handling stress and persist through uncertainty.

What does this seismic shift in global Macro and Meta and Micro Mindsets mean for us?

We believe this represents an opportunity to be on the cause side of this shift rather than waiting passively on the effect side. We are all potential leaders who play an essential role in furthering mindset change. Although people say that the economy and the market are beyond our control and limit our choices, it is the leaders and people in their companies whose mindset determines what is possible. This is where our roles as mindset shapers, or "mindsetters" come in. Our generation is dealing with unprecedented amounts of uncertainty and anxiety brought about by issues like pandemics, war, climate change, and economic disruptions. During such times, as psychologist Viktor Frankl pointed out back in 1945, we cannot survive without finding meaning. Finding meaning in MindsetMap terms involves connecting to our passion and vision while engaging our unique competencies and genius in the form of a mission. This has to then be supported by clear and ambitious goals and a sense of our role within our larger context.

As we have shared with you, our findings show that exceptional performance requires a very solid Meta Mindset where "ego" and "soul" are in balance. It also demands an aligned Macro Mindset to keep us going and guide us on the way as we take daily action guided by our Micro Mindset. As they say, "all roads lead to Rome" – change starts inside with the strength and clarity of our own mindset rather than in the outside world. Once our mindset is aligned, the potential role of a mindsetter for others opens to us. We strongly believe that each person using the MindsetMap Inventory has the potential for a quiet but powerful form of inner revolution. In our work, every day we see how mindset matters most for the actions that our clients take towards achieving their goals. Hence, we want to invite you to be part of this mindset change movement as a messenger, catalyst, and instigator.

AFTERWORD FOR MINDSETTERS

As outlined in the Closing Reflections chapter, our vision for the MindsetMap is that it will become a vehicle to create the only true revolution – the revolution of the mind. We call it a revolution as it requires an awakening to the realization that we are all connected systemically, and so are our minds.

Global mindset change requires a higher level of consciousness, and many mindsetters take this vehicle to business executives, entrepreneurs, political leaders, and others in leadership roles. We believe the MindsetMap Inventory has a great potential to help all those in leadership positions to have a visual map of their mindset and understand where and how they need to align, adjust and evolve it.

Mindsetters are the coaches and leaders we train and equip with the MindsetMap tool so that they can integrate it into their practice. We already have growing number of coaches and leaders, as HR professionals, internal consultants, and leaders around the globe, who share our vision and are using this tool to help shape the mindsets that will create the future.

We hope you enjoyed this book about the MindsetMap approach, methodology, and toolbox.

- If you are a coach or consultant, you may now be interested in learning more about how to bring the MindsetMap into your work.

- If you are in a role dealing with learning and growth, leadership development, or talent management, you might be wondering about using the MindsetMap.

- Or you could be an entrepreneur or an intrapreneur leader exploring how to lead your team to the next level by helping them align their mindsets for the best possible results, both as individuals and as a team.

In all three cases, we have good news for you. We have created a training program called the MindsetMap™ Coach Certification which runs yearly in English and is now also available in Greek, French, Italian, Japanese, and Spanish. You can find more information about our programs on our webpage at https://www.mindsetmapsinternational.com/certification. This six-module certification program has fifty hours of hybrid (online and interactive) learning that helps professionals become familiar with the tool to apply it in their coaching work or leadership. If you wish to learn more, please contact us at office@mindsetmaps.com.

If you are interested in exploring your mindset, you can try our inventory. There is a simplified "taster" version on this link: https://www.mindsetmaps.com/test/meta

At the end, you will have a taste of your Meta Mindset, and find ways to get in touch with the certified MindsetMaps coach of your choice, get access to the full inventory, and work through the next steps to achieve your outcomes.

If you are interested in learning more about MindsetMaps and the power of mindset, you can go to Mickey's blog on *Psychology Today*: https://www.psychologytoday.com/us/blog/purpose/202203/the-war-your-attention/.

We also have our mindset mastery blog on our website here: https://www.mindsetmapsinternational.com/mindsetmasteryblog.

Finally, join us on Instagram, Facebook, and LinkedIn as a mindsetter!

Our handles and addresses are:

- @Mindsetmaps_mindsetters **on Insta.**
- toSuccessMindsetmaps **on Facebook**
- MindsetMaps International **on LinkedIn**

BIOGRAPHIES

Robert Dilts has been a developer, author, trainer and consultant in the field of Neuro-Linguistic Programming (NLP) – a model of human learning and communication – since its creation in 1975 by John Grinder and Richard Bandler. Robert is also co-developer (with his brother John Dilts) of Success Factor Modeling and (with Stephen Gilligan)of the process of Generative Change. A long time student and colleague of both Grinder and Bandler, Mr. Dilts also studied personally with Milton H. Erickson, M.D. and Gregory Bateson.

In addition to spearheading the applications of NLP to education, creativity, health, and leadership, his personal contributions to the field of NLP include much of the seminal work on the NLP techniques of Strategies and Belief Systems, and the development of what has be- come known as Systemic NLP. An author more than 30 books, some of his techniques and models include: Reimprinting, the Disney Imagineering Strategy, Integration of Conflicting Beliefs, Sleight of Mouth Patterns, The Spelling Strategy, The Allergy Technique, Neuro-Logical Levels, The Belief Change Cycle, The SFM Circle of Success and the Six Steps of Generative Coaching (with Stephen Gilligan).

Past corporate clients and sponsors have included Apple Inc., Microsoft, Hewlett-Packard, IBM, Société Générale, Bank of America, The World Bank, Alitalia, Telecom Italia, RAI Italia, Lucasfilms Ltd., Ernst & Young, AT Kearney, Salomon, The American Society for Training and Development, EDHEC Business School and the State Railway of Italy. He has lectured extensively on coaching, leadership, organizational learning and change management, making presentations and keynote addresses for The International Coaching Federation (ICF), HEC Paris, The United Nations, The European Forum for Quality Management, The World Health Organization, The Milton H. Erickson Foundation, Harvard University and the International University of Monaco. In 1997 and 1998, Robert supervised the design of *Tools for Living,* the behavior management portion of the program used by *Weight Watcher's International.*

A co-founder of Dilts Strategy Group, Robert is also co-founder of NLP University International, the Institute for Advanced Studies of Health (IASH) and the International Association for Generative Change (IAGC). Robert has a degree in Behavioral Technology from the University of California at Santa Cruz.

Mickey A. Feher is a Hungarian-American based in New York who works internationally as a coach, generative consultant and facilitator. He is the co-founder of MindsetMaps International with Robert B. Dilts and the co-creator of the Success MindsetMap™ Inventory. He is an active member of the leadership team of the Dilts Strategy Group. He also serves as the CEO of Purpose & Company, an international organizational development company active globally. Previously he served as the Executive Director for The International Association for Generative Change, a global organization founded by Robert Dilts and Steve Gilligan. Before becoming a coach, he had a distinguished business career and served in various executive level roles across Europe in multinational companies such as Deutsche Telekom, Aegis/Synovate and he was a senior consultant at Deloitte.

As an organizational development consultant and team and executive business coach he has worked with clients like Microsoft, Bayer, BNP-Paribas, ING, GE, KRAFT/MONDELEZ, EDF and many medium size and start-up companies.

His passion and higher purpose are to help others find meaning in their life and reach exceptional results. He is the co-author of the book Generative Consulting, Tools for creativity, consciousness and collective transformation and a regular contributor in Psychology Today and Forbes. He is also a regular speaker at international conferences like the International NLP Conference by ANLP, Global NLP Summit and NLP Masters recently. He is a father of two, who practices martial arts, yoga and meditation every day.

One of his special interests is changing the imbalance of the feminine and masculine principles in leadership which includes working with men to redefine healthy masculinity in all roles men play in life. To this end he founded the MANTORSHIFT Podcast which is now focusing on how mindset is the basis of exceptional performance and purpose driven impact.

Mickey has an MA in organizational psychology and an MBA in international management from Case Western University of Cleveland. He is a Master Practitioner; Consultant and Trainer certified by NLPU and a Generative Coach certified by the IAGC and is a qualified trainer of the Success Factor Modelling volumes I-III.

BIBLIOGRAPHY AND REFERENCES

Bezos, J., Jobs, S., et al (2014), *50 Entrepreneurs Share Priceless Advice*: YouTube.

Crum, A. J., Salovey, P., & Achor, S. (2013). *Rethinking Stress: The Role of Mindsets in Determining the Stress Response*: Journal of Personality and Social Psychology.

Colata, Gina (2021), *Kati Kariko Helped Shield the World From the Coronavirus*, The New York Times.

Deutschman, A. (2001), *The Second Coming of Steve Jobs*, New York, Crown Business.

Dilts, R., Feher, M., Falcone, E., Normandeau, C., Thiriet, J. F., Wyss, K. (2020), *Generative Consulting: Tools for creativity, consciousness and collective transformation*, Santa Cruz, CA: Dilts Strategy Group.

Dilts, R. (2015), *Success Factor Modeling, Vol. I: Next Generation Entrepreneurs – Live Your Dream and Make a Better World Through Your Business*, Santa Cruz, CA: Dilts Strategy Group.

Dilts, R. (2016), *Success Factor Modeling, Vol. II: Generative Collaboration – Releasing the Creative Power of Collective Intelligence*, Santa Cruz, CA: Dilts Strategy Group.

Dilts, R. (2017), *Success Factor Modeling, Volume III – Conscious Leadership and Resilience: Orchestrating Innovation and Fitness for the Future*, Santa Cruz, CA: Dilts Strategy Group.

Dilts, R. & Gilligan, S. (2021), *Generative Coaching Volume 1: The Journey of Creative and Sustainable Change*, Santa Cruz, CA: International Association for Generative Change.

Dilts, R. (2003), *From Coach to Awakener*, Santa Cruz, CA: Dilts Strategy Group.

Dweck, C. S., & Leggett, E. L. (1988), *A social-cognitive approach to motivation and personality*: Psychological Review.

Dweck, C. (2017), *Mindset: Changing the way you think to fulfill your potential*, London, UK: Robinson.

Dupeyrat, C., & Mariné, C. (2005). *Implicit Theories of Intelligence, Goal Orientation, Cognitive Engagement, and Achievement: A Test of Dweck's Model with Returning to School Adults*: Contemporary Educational Psychology.

Feher, M. (2021). *Mindset: Your Leash or Your Wings*: Forbes.

Feher, M. (2022). *The Intrapreneur Mindset: Why organizations should pay more attention to mindset*: Psychology Today.

Feher, M. (2022). *The War for Your Attention: Are you in charge of your mind?*: Psychology Today.

French, R. P. I. (2016), *The fuzziness of mindsets: Divergent conceptualizations and characterizations of mindset theory and praxis*; International Journal of Organizational Analysis.

Friedman, Milton (1970) *A Friedman doctrine-- The Social Responsibility Of Business Is to Increase Its Profits*, The New York Times.

Gollwitzer, P. M. (2011), *Mindset Theory of Action Phases*. In P. A. M. V. Lange, A. W. Kruglanski, & E. T. Higgins (Eds.), *Handbook of Theories of Social Psychology: Volume One*, Los Angeles: SAGE Social Psychology Program.

Isaacson, W. (2011), *Steve Jobs*, New York: Simon and Schuster.

Jobs, S., (2005). *Stanford Commencement Address*: YouTube.

Jung, C. G. (1921, 1971). *Psychological Types*, Collected Works of C.G. Jung, vol. 6. Princeton, NJ: Princeton University Press.

Kariko, Katalin Dr. (2022) Excerpts from Dr. Karikó's acceptance speech at VinFuture Grand Prize from the VinFuture Foundation an at Hanoi, April 28th, 2021 and when receiving the inaugural VinFuture Grand Prize.

Kelley, D., & Kelley, T. (2015), *Creative Confidence: Unleashing the Creative Potential Within Us All*, New York: HarperCollins Publishers.

Kollewe Julia, (2020), *Covid vaccine technology pioneer: 'I never doubted it would work'*, The Guardian.

Lukianoff, G. and Haidt, J. (2018), *The Coddling of the American Mind*. New York: Penguin Publishing Group.

Maio, G. and Haddoc, G. (2018), *The Psychology of Attitudes and Attitude Change, Thousand Oaks, CA: SAGE Publications, Ltd.*

McCrae, R. R., & Costa, P. T. (1987). *Validation of the five-factor model of personality across instruments and observers: Journal of Personality and Social Psychology.*

Mehregany, M. (2018), *Innovation for Engineers*, New York: Springer International Publishing.

Meier, J. D., and Kropp, M. (2010), *Getting Results the Agile Way: A Personal Results System for Work and Life.* Bellevue, WA: Innovation Playhouse.

Obikoya, Jeremiah, (2022) Intrapreneur – What you need to know about an intrapreneur, The Youth Initiative for Economic Empowerment (YIEE).

Ratchford, E., et al (2021), *Mindset as Characteristic Adaptations: Using Response Surface Analysis to Assess Mindset in the Personality System:* Frontiers in Psychology.

Rogers, C. (1995), *On Becoming a Person: A Therapist's View of Psychotherapy*, Boston, MA: Houghton Mifflin Harcourt.

Sample Ian, (2021) *Scientists' egos are key barrier to progress, says Covid vaccine pioneer*, The Guardian.

Sternberg, R. J. (2019), *Enhancing People's Creativity*; In J. C. Kaufman & R. J. Sternberg (Eds.), *The Cambridge Handbook of Creativity* (2nd ed.): Cambridge University Press.

Vogel, T. and Wänke, M. (2016), *Attitudes and Attitude Change*, East Sussex, England: Psychology Press.

Weber, H. (2021), *Cognitive Processes in Design Thinking Optimization of perception, processing, and reasoning*, Dissertation for IADE - Faculdade de Design, Tecnologia e Comunicação – Universidade Europeia.

Winfrey, O. (2019), *The Path Made Clear: Discovering Your Life's Direction and Purpose*, New York: Flatiron Books.

Young, J. & Simon, W. (2006), *iCon Steve Jobs: The Greatest Second Act in the History of Business*, New Delhi: Wiley India.

Zion, S. and Crum, A. (2018), *Mindsets Matter: A New Framework for Harnessing the Placebo Effect in Modern Medicine*: International Review of Neurobiology.